TRIUMPH BONNEVILLE

John Nelson

CONTENTS

FOREWORD	4
HISTORY	5
EVOLUTION	10
SPECIFICATION	13
ROAD TESTS	18
OWNER'S VIEW	25
BUYING	29
CLUBS, SPECIALISTS & BOOKS	31
PHOTO GALLERY	33

Foulis

Haynes

ISBN 0 85429 453 8

A FOULIS Motorcycling Book

First published 1985

© Haynes Publishing Group

All rights reserved. No part of this book may be reproduced or transmitted in any form or by any means, electronic or mechanical, including photocopying, recording or by any information storage or retrieval system, without written permission from the publisher.

Published by:
Haynes Publishing Group
Sparkford, Yeovil,
Somerset BA22 7JJ

Haynes Publications Inc.
861 Lawrence Drive, Newbury Park, California 91320 USA

British Library Cataloguing in Publication Data

Nelson, John R.
  Triumph Bonneville.—(Super Profile)
  1. Triumph Bonneville motorcycle—History
  I. Title   II. Series
  629.2'275   TL448.T7
  ISBN 0-85429-453-8

Dust jacket design: Rowland Smith
Jacket colour illustration: The National Motorcycle Museum
Page Layout: Peter Kay
Photographs: Andrew Morland, Wright Richardson Associates
Road Tests: The Motor Cycle, courtesy of EMAP National Press Ltd
Printed in England by:
J.H. Haynes & Co Ltd

Titles in the *Super Profile* series

Ariel Square Four (F388)
BMW R69 & R69S (F387)
Brough Superior SS100 (F364)
BSA A7 & A10 (F446)
BSA Bantam (F333)
Honda CB750 sohc (F351)
International Norton (F365)
KSS Velocette (F444)
Matchless G3L & G80 (F455)
MV Agusta America (F334)
Norton Commando (F335)
Sunbeam S7 & S8 (F363)
Triumph Thunderbird (F353)
Triumph Trident (F352)
Vincent Twins (F460)
AC/Ford/Shelby Cobra (F381)
Austin-Healey 'Frogeye' Sprite (F343)
Chevrolet Corvette (F432)
Ferrari 250GTO (F308)
Fiat X1/9 (F341)
Ford Cortina 1600E (F310)
Ford GT40 (F332)
Jaguar E-Type (F370)
Jaguar D-Type & XKSS (F371)
Jaguar Mk 2 Saloons (F307)
Jaguar SS90 & SS100 (F372)
Lancia Stratos (F340)
Lotus Elan (F330)
Lotus Seven (F385)
MGB (F305)
MG Midget & Austin-Healey Sprite (except 'Frogeye') (F344)
Mini Cooper (F445)
Morris Minor Series MM (F412)
Morris Minor & 1000 (ohv) (F331)
Porsche 911 Carrera (F311)
Rolls-Royce Corniche (F411)
Triumph Stag (F342)

Bell U-H1 (F437)
B29 Superfortress (F339)
Boeing 707 (F356)
Grumman F8F Bearcat (F447)
Harrier (F357)
Hawker Hunter (F448)
MIG 21 (F439)
Mosquito (F422)
Phantom II (F376)
P51 Mustang (F423)
Sea King (F377)
SEPECAT Jaguar (F438)
Super Etendard (F378)
Tiger Moth (F421)
Vulcan (F436)

Great Western Kings (F426)
Intercity 125 (F428)
V2 'Green Arrow' Class (F427)

Further titles in this series will be published at regular intervals. For information on new titles please contact your bookseller or write to the publisher.

Super Profile

FOREWORD

It was in 1948 as a direct result of the purchase of a Triumph Speed Twin, resplendent in its post-war finish of Amaranth Red and bright chrome, that, as an eager motorcycling graduate engineer, I was persuaded that a company capable of producing such an advanced and competent product so soon after the cessation of the hostilities of World War Two was surely the sort of organisation to which I had long wished to belong to earn my living.

During the next twenty years the company developed and prospered, becoming one of the manufacturing and exporting giants of the day. Many successes were achieved in that time, not the least of which was the predominance of Triumph as the police motorcycle in over two hundred military, police and official organisations throughout the world, including behind the Iron Curtain. The consistent reliability gained in the International Six Days, Welsh and Big Bear or Catalina types of competitive event is witnessed by the Gold, Silver and Bronze medals, vases, trophies and cups, year following year, won by many of the models in the production range. The world's fastest for over a decade is no mean achievement in itself!

However, the Bonneville story as it has unfolded for nearly 25 years has become inevitably woven as an integral part of the overall Triumph tapestry, and forms the subject of this book.

Having spent an extremely happy five years in charge of the Triumph Experimental and Development Department, I accepted the next seemingly logical move to the appointment of World Service Manager (as the Americans dubbed it) and from this chair witnessed the birth, growth and, in effect, the gradual maturing of the Bonneville. It's a good story, packed with success, action, life and drama, but perhaps, like many a good love story, may not have the inevitable happy ending.

Although the original Triumph Engineering Company Limited has long since vanished, it is with considerable pleasure that I wish to record the gratitude I have experienced in having been able to call on my previous Triumph colleagues to remind and prompt me of those earlier days, during the preparation of this book.

Principally I would acknowledge the help of Harry Wooldridge in more than just extremely well-informed proof reading, but, even more importantly, the provision of the essential and previously missing technical details drawn from his own personal records during the time of the Co-operative. Also I must record my thanks to Ivor Davies for the use of his own private historical records and for the use of his all-embracing supply of Triumph photographs and memorabilia.

Tremendous help has always been available from Tony Cooper of TMS Nottingham, and from Chris Wright, who kindly took the photograph for the cover, and many others appearing throughout this book.

Finally, and in more permanent salute to the memory of the development of the Bonneville, I wish to acknowledge the kind assistance given by Roy Richards in the provision of the 1959 'Bonnie' from his vast collection of beautifully restored British motorcycles, now finally on display at the new National Motorcycle Museum at Bickenhill in Warwickshire.

John. R. Nelson.

Super Profile

HISTORY

There will be few who doubt that the Triumph Bonneville model fulfilled the advertising claim of the day in having become 'A legend in its own time'. Perhaps of even greater significance is the fact that it is surely destined to be one of the more outstanding landmarks in the history of manufacture and production of the British motorcycle industry.

As an added distinction, and unlike many of its predecessors or even its contemporaries, the actual arrival of the Bonneville on the scene was neither the final product of a specific design project, nor was it even the outcome of a planned routine development programme. It was the achievement of that inevitable culmination point in the progressive evolution of a pre-1939 war design, which in the light of subsequent commercial experience has proven to have been fundamentally correct in its original concept, and was successfully and progressively guided and channelled to the ultimate of its development.

Previous Triumph model series such as the Tiger Cub, Tigress, Twenty-One and 5TA Speed-Twin, or even the ill-fated Tina Scooter, were the materialization of an original design concept, painstakingly detailed through subsequent development and testing to the final production stage. But not so the Bonneville.

Totally contemporary with the arrival of the Bonneville in 1959 was the Issigonis Mini, and now equally long in the tooth! Nevertheless, here we have a total contrast. The Mini was the achievement of a vision of the integration of revolutionary engineering images into a brand new concept, from the original egg-shaped monocoque body shell and transverse engine to the unique rubber-mounted sub-frame and associated rubber/hydrolastic suspension in conjunction with the previously unheard-of small wheels. It was designed as the 'Mini' from the first centre line on the drawing board to the 'First-off' down the production line, breaking entirely new ground and all traditions in its journey to successful fruition.

Perhaps we labour the point, but this illustrates the contrast in that the Bonneville was created by an altogether different process, and arrived at by a completely different route. No clean sheet of paper here, and most certainly no new centre-line or design concept. And yet so successful! It could almost be claimed that the Bonneville had the doubtful distinction of not having been thought of until its actual unwelcome arrival, and could even be best described as never having been conceived at all!

There were those who claimed it was surreptitiously and quietly hatched, but in this particular instance, the hatch is as in 'plot'! There's a grain of truth here too! The technical staff at the Triumph Engineering Co. Ltd., based subsequent to the immediate post-war move from Coventry at the new factory situated in the 'Green Belt' near the village of Meriden, between Coventry and Birmingham, had always had a close working liaison with their own worldwide distributor network. In the motorcycle business, this inevitably was coupled with lifelong personal associations, and this particularly applied to the very active East and West US Distributorships. They were part of a close knit, high pressure team, headed by Edward Turner, who had perforce to develop a special sort of self-preservation by ensuring they individually maintained a sensitive finger on the prevailing market pulse whilst staying closely in tune with their dynamic leader. All were more than fully aware that the name of the game in the late 1950s was more performance year by year to keep ahead of the competition.

The years from 1955 to 1957 had occupied the Triumph factory experimental and development department not only with the 350/500cc 3TA and 5TA Model 'Twenty One' and 'Speed Twin' project, together with the introduction of the revolutionary AC generator system, but also with Terriers, Scooters (including a 200cc two-stroke twin cylinder, variable-speed belt drive scooter that eventually became the Tigress), and the tiresome Tiger Cubs.

One of this series of developments was the very successful single carburettor, swinging arm 42 bhp Tiger 110 model, a 117 mph road sports version of its famous predecessor, the 650cc Thunderbird. The T110 had been unveiled in 1957, 'so what more do they want?' was the Edward Turner theme at the time.

His classic and oft quoted responses to returning researchers from trips abroad, or during a high level sales meeting following the presentation of a well-prepared and persuasive project for the future, amounted to ..... 'I will tell them what they can have .... my boy!' Such was the power and control of the man, and the situation in the market place of the day.

At this point we had better go back to the beginning and explain that in 1936, when Edward Turner had been invited by Jack Sangster, (whose family owned the Ariel Factory at the time) to join him as

Super Profile

Chief Designer of the newly-formed Triumph Engineering Company Ltd., at Dale Street, in Coventry, his declared objective was to design and produce a motorcycle to achieve twenty thousand miles 'from the end of the production line' with no more attention than the specified maintenance scheduled, and with absolutely no mechanical troubles whatsoever (still a rare occurrence in those days).

During the whole of the period of his control of Triumph, although interested in the achievements of others in competitive events, and 'out and out' racing in particular, he was strictly not at all interested in any form of factory participation in high speed competition. Any attempt by factory personnel to convert or utilise the factory facilities and resources to aid the outside world in such adventures was strictly 'verboten'.

Not to say Edward did not enjoy his visits to the Isle of Man during TT week, or even the Manx Grand Prix. It was, in fact, on one of these visits that he unexpectedly walked slap-bang into two of his own technical staff weighing in a T100 racing machine, clandestinely prepared within the factory for the Senior Event. It evoked the famous, yet infamous response to the question 'That's nicely prepared, whose is it?' 'It's ours Sir!' which resulted in the culprit being consigned to duties in Saudi Arabia within weeks of the crime.

However, not all were discouraged by the set-backs and stonewalling, and were often spurred on by their own burning convictions. The overall effect was a continuously active scene of pressing forward towards further progress, improvement and development. In retrospect, this consolidated devotion to the product did contribute to an inexorable progress in a forward direction, and, we suspect, Edward Turner quietly fed and thrived on it.

The policy held by Triumph for Meriden and the UK had little or no effect on the independent enthusiasm of either the East or West coast US Corporations. Both were doing their own thing in their individual ways to wrest increasing power from the original 650cc Thunderbird twin, and latterly, from the 1957 T110.

As both these models stemmed directly, and in natural sequence, from the original 1938 5T Speed Twin and T100 Tiger 100 Models (the latter having been offered in 1946 wth the additional availability of a factory racing kit — solely for the genuine enthusiast to purchase separately, and fit for himself — 'using his own superlative skill'), the original super 'N' camshafts, the later 'Q' cams and racing cam-followers intended for the T100 were still available and were found to work wonders for the Thunderbird.

American ingenuity being what it is, this only whetted voracious appetites for performance and power, and the dear old yanks were already progressing from their local number six grinds on their needle roller bearinged camshafts and followers, through to the really hot number nines, requiring specially-wound non-surge racing valve springs and seven degree inlet ports together with all the lightening and strengthening that ensued.

The days of over-the-counter racers, and factory-developed single purpose racing machinery had not yet dawned, but the American racing brigade had already appreciated that the Triumph 650cc twin engine would readily respond to individualistic developments and local tuning expertise.

Right across the USA the tuners were gas flowing cylinder heads, developing exotic ignition systems and exhaust equipment to join the competitive fight to claim the number one spot in local and national competitive events. Again with the assistance of the Triumph Corporation in Baltimore, and the conspiratorial supply of components from the factory, these individual efforts culminated in the magnificent achievement of Jack Wilson's tuned streamliner, fitted with a basically standard but 'breathed-on' 650cc twin cylinder Triumph Thunderbird engine ridden by an intrepid Johnny Allan, achieving the first Triumph World's Speed Record on two wheels of 214.47 mph on the Bonneville salt flats on the 6th September, 1956.

This success really did rock the factory back on its heels. So it could done! A pre-war designed Triumph engine could still be tuned to break and hold the World's Speed Record on two wheels, and that record was the average speed held over a measured mile!

Imagine the next visit to England of the two US distributor Presidents. Bursting with pride of achievement, and it certainly was no mean performance, bringing with them the acclaim of the crowned and acknowledged leaders of the US competitive motorcycle field, and the huge potential prospect of ever increasing sales now within their grasp.

Two very happy Presidents, Bill Johnson of Johnson Motors Inc. Pasadena (not the later successful Bill Johnson of the 1962 224.57 mph World's Speed Record streamliner fame; he was a truck driver extraordinaire at that time) and Denis McCormack, late of Coventry, UK, were both old enough and wise enough not to lose heart at the predictable Edward Turner lack of apparent enthusiasm for their enterprises or their inevitable requests for support in the provision of yet higher performance ex-works factory-made catalogue models.

The Distributor Competition Departments at the premises of both East and West Coast US Distributorships comprised in the main each of the Service Departments' own freelance activity at the weekends. In supporting their dealer network participation in local events, the success of their endeavours was correlated and fed back to the lower echelons at the factory, and during routine visits to the UK the key personnel never left the UK without fully appraising the interested residents of Meriden of the latest developments on the US scene. During this period in the mid and late 1950s, competition on the UK race tracks for what is now classified as Production Class racing was gathering momentum, so both privateer and club entrants were continually pressing and pestering the factory for tuning assistance, advice and new developments.

Coincidentally, the oil companies were researching and producing their new ranges of additives (remember ICA?) which allowed higher octanes, higher compression ratios and higher bearing loadings with less wear. Torque and bhp began to climb.

It was in 1958, whilst Charles Grandfield was Chief Engineer at Triumph, that a test bed project was put in hand to test to destruction a brand new one-piece forged crankshaft with a bolt-on flywheel. (The previous pre-war designed three-piece version had started to indicate its inability to provide the greater duty inevitably to be demanded of it.) To obtain the further required boost in power required for this evaluation, a Tiger 100 twin carburettor splayed inlet port cylinder head was suitably modified to fit a-top the T110, and run on a straight-through exhaust system.

The endurance test was completed with flying colours, and following a strip down and examination, the engine was rebuilt and prepared for the next test, which was to consist of routine road testing and speed checks at the MIRA Proving Ground at Lindley. It will be understood this was utterly normal routine day-to-day development and testing work, but Frank Baker, then in charge of the Experimental Department, had an additional twinkle in his eye.

This twin carburettor T110 flying test bed was more than the answer to an incipient problem; it was to be the answer to a maiden's prayer!

Normally, a pre-production prototype is a deliberately undistinguished and suitably disguised test bike, but this time it was built with full Paint and Polishing Shop participation. The nacelle, twin carburettors, competition magneto, short dropped angle straight handlebars, remote rubber-mounted float chambers and narrow twinseat made it look every inch a real thoroughbred. A twin carburettor T110! It deserved a better designation than that!

When invited by Frank for an official viewing in the presence of his senior staff, Edward Turner used the opportunity to deliver a grave, on-the-spot commercial lecture, ending with the forbidding yet prophetic threat directed towards Frank Baker that this particular project would lead to bankruptcy! It took more than twenty five years to put down the Bonnie – but that's another story yet to unfold.

No decision had been taken by October, 1958 with the November Earls Court annual Motor Cycle Show already having been planned down to the last detail, and even the glossy catalogues printed. Reluctantly, but mainly to please those durned Americans, an additional model was added to the range, a twin carburettor Tiger 110 model. At last, a decision – **THE** decision was made, in honour of Johnny Allan and that day on the Salt Flats in Utah – 'Bonneville' was to be its name.

The machine went into production almost immediately following the Show, the first models being finished in two-tone Pearl Grey and Tangerine, the remainder of the painted parts being in traditional Black, including the twin seat cover, lined only with a single piping band. However, halfway through the season this scheme was changed to commonise with the Export version to Royal Blue, replacing the Tangerine (lower tank half), and with the oil tank and battery/tool box now also in Pearl Grey. A narrow single level twinseat and deletion of the 'dropped handlebars' in favour of the standard 'English touring bar' were the only other changes to be made.

For 1960 the nacelle was dropped in favour of a separate chromed headlamp and telescopic fork rubber gaiters, and for the first time an alternator replaced the familiar dynamo on a sports machine, although the Lucas K2F auto advance magneto was retained. A new lightweight duplex cradle frame was introduced which was quickly amended prior to 1961 to incorporate additional stiffening members to overcome a frame breakage problem. Fully-floating single leading shoes arrived on front and rear brakes to cope with the increased performance. 1960 also saw the introduction of a T120C (US) competition version, with high level exhaust pipes and silencers, trials universal tyres and a detachable headlight. The following year saw the remote carburettor float bowl between the original 'chopped off' Monobloc carburettors replaced by standard $1\frac{1}{16}$ inch choke Amal Monoblocs. A Lucas Red Label K2F or K2FC magneto continued to be fitted to this model until coil ignition with twin contact breakers was introduced in 1963.

1962 however, saw a basic engine change from a 50% engine balance factor to that of 71% and then 85%, in an effort to reduce the inherent vibration aggravated by

Super Profile

the increased power output to the catalogue-claimed 46 bhp. The discontinuation of the quickly detachable headlamp feature, obviating the unpredictable 'quick detach' trick of the electrical feed plug whilst negotiating the sharpest corners on the darkest night, was welcomed by experienced riders, who consequently had given this feature the deserved accolade of 'Prince of Darkness'.

The next progressive change introducing the long awaited unit-construction of engine, transmission and gearbox occurred in 1963, and was accompanied by an entirely new single downtube frame. This, we suspect, was the genuine Edward Turner 'Bonneville', specifically designed for the next decade and replacing the unofficial 1959 intruder that had burst its way into the programme in natural response to the company's own inherent momentum. But so much changed from the original established design in the 1963 version that many said that the character of the first Bonneville was now lost for ever. The new version was more compact and tidier, and the riding position and roadholding was so much more taut and precise, that a new yardstick of comparison had been achieved.

These changes, although accompanied by some inevitable minor service problems, proved the basic soundness of the design, as indeed was witnessed by the minimal fundamental engineering changes in design year by year until the hand of Umberslade began to appear in 1970. Before then, and to suit this revised version of the T120 model, a new range of high performance components began to appear including the very latest in current technology — Nimonic exhaust valves which were made available for the production race enthusiasts. This type of 500 mile endurance race began as the Dunholme 500 in the immediate post-war years on an abandoned Lincolnshire aerodrome circuit (from which the writer once flew in an Armstrong Whitworth Whitley aircraft — and almost certainly the 1966 Bonneville fully equipped with all the available gear was faster down the runway!).

In these competitive events, Triumph reigned supreme for a number of successive years, and although the factory design and development departments were not actively involved in the preparation or production of ready-made, over-the-counter racing machines, the racing regulations for these type of events gradually introduced us all to a new word, that of homologation. In effect this meant that a specified number of factory production-made machines had to be certified by the factory to have actually been catalogued, made and sold to the exact specification of the entrant's machine. So for the first time, and in the wake of worldwide competition success, the Thruxton Bonneville was produced down the factory assembly track against dealer orders. The sad fact that all the high performance parts being manufactured for distribution through the Service and Spares Department were instantly collared by production, and not replaced for nigh on a full season, was of little importance to all except the privateer, but great stuff for the dealers.

By 1964 even the standard production Bonneville had Nimonic exhaust valves and $1\frac{1}{8}$ inch choke carburettors, but the most important improvement for all Triumph riders arrived in 1966 when twelve volt Zener diode-controlled electrical systems were introduced. No more 'switch controlled — to balance generator output' circuits. No more emergency start switches, and at last energy transfer died its not untimely death. From this point to the end of 1969, the 650 Triumph Bonneville had achieved its peak of performance in both sales throughput and customer satisfaction.

Throughout this period, the USA continued to import their own variants of East and West Coast models for both road and track, including the 'TT' model, a short circuit racing model with straight through exhaust, stripped of lights and devoid of comfort, which dominated the US competition scene for all these years.

There remains little doubt that the 1969 vintage was to be the best year of the complete 650 cc range, including the Bonneville itself. At that time it was the ultimate ideal of every young motorcyclist, and his dream motorcycle.

But fundamental changes were afoot. Edward Turner, the original driving force and guardian of the Triumph conception, was no longer at the helm. New management structure had been built on the foundations of BSA/Triumph integration, and the future research and model development transferred to the Umberslade Hall Research Centre was coming to fruition with its first crop of new model designs. It was reported that the Bonneville for the 70s was to be included amongst them.

Enough has been written elsewhere to record the disaster this was to prove to be for BSA, Meriden, and the Bonneville in particular, through which staunch attempts were to be made by the men of Meriden to pick their way through the over-tall and breaking frames, and the headlamps held on with chromed bent wire.

Despite the introduction in 1973 of a much heralded 750 cc-disc front brake version of the Bonneville, by February 1974 the design changes incorporated in an impossible attempt to maintain marketability of the whole range had failed to help prevent the inevitable failure of the BSA Parent Organisation, and the consequent closure of Meriden, despite Government intervention and the involvement of Norton.

A history of the Bonneville

Super Profile

must inevitably record here that it was at this point that the workforce at Meriden decreed that the Bonneville had not deserved to die – even though at this time it had reached the ripe old age of fifteen! (and goodness, so had the Mini). Through a series of 'sit-ins', blockades, to an Act of Parliament, and from 'piracy' to legitimacy, a co-operative was finally officially formed in 1974, and although heavily under-financed, recommenced production of the 650-750 cc Bonneville in April, 1975. These machines, now of US legal necessity, incorporated left footshift gearchange mechanism, 5 speed gears and a rear disc brake.

1977 was the 25th Jubilee year of the reign of Her Majesty Queen Elizabeth II, and in celebration (at the direct suggestion of Lord Stokes) a commemorative and certificated strictly limited edition of a red, white and blue-lined Silver Jubilee model version of the Bonneville was produced, 1000 for the home market, with 1000 US variants for the North American continent. Additionally, the primary gearbox and timing covers were very heavily chromium plates, setting off the silver grey twinseat with smart red piping. Many are still preserved in their original wrappings as a future investment. Some are still kept meticulously clean and polished in the front parlour, and one is known to be kept totally sealed in yacht varnish by its original owner!

Triumph in its export activities to many overseas markets had always had to keep ahead of legislative requirements in the affected countries. To some it meant keeping the importer supported with facilities to cope with the local problems himself, such as the re-wiring facility to provide 'headlights on if engine running' – such as Canada in 1978. In other markets homologation was proving to be the dreaded word. This often meant the submission of the complete machine to the central investigatory testing station of the country in question, such as the TUV authority in Germany with full certification needed in respect of that countries' own pertinent legal and constructional requirements before any licence granting importation and distribution rights would be granted.

None however had ever been so tough as the US Environmental Protection Agency (EPA) anti-pollution requirements for 1978. At the very least the approved procedure for each machine submitted for certification and approval testing took about 10 days of 24 hours supervised continual routine start/stop and minimum to maximum running performance, to complete approximately 10,000 miles. During this period it needed to be completely untouched by spanners or screwdrivers – except for strictly observed compliance with the published Servicing Schedules – after which samples of exhaust gases were taken, which had to be proved to comply with absolute critical minimal requirements for carbon monoxide, hydrocarbons and nitrous oxide content – using completely sealed and tamperproof carburettors.

Thus evolved the T140E Model, 'E' simply indicating successful emission compliance, otherwise the traditional and lucrative US market would have been closed for ever.

Two more fundamental changes were to be made to the T140V Bonneville model before it was to cease production at Meriden, its original place of birth and development. In 1981, the luxury of an electric starter was added, and although reasonably successful when considered it had been grafted onto an already elderly design of engine, it did ultimately provide the reliability expected of it.

The last development was in many ways an interesting and potentially successful variant, although possibly more of an economical exercise to squeeze a few more drops of commercial viability from the failing liquidity of the co-operative experiment. A 650 cc version was re-introduced, with the resurrected name of Thunderbird. (In 1951 the Ford Motor Company of America had formally asked the Triumph Engineering Company for permission to use this very same name for their product, prior to the launch of their Thunderbird model). This 650 cc model was a pretty version in blue, but sadly it heralded the closure only too soon of the Meriden factory, to be followed rapidly by the auction and disposal of all manufacturing facilities. Within days the ultimate indignity had occurred, when the factory itself was razed to the ground to make way for a housing estate.

Thus ended the longest running British production motorcycle series ever recorded, from 1938 as a 'B' range 500 cc twin cylinder model to the final 1983 'B' range 750 cc model. A number of components fitted in the first were still used 45 years later in the last, from the oil pump driving block to the gear change selectors, and from the rockers to the tappet guide blocks.

Perhaps in memory, and just as a tribute, one of the roads on the new Meriden housing estate may be named Bonneville Crescent!

9

Super Profile

EVOLUTION

The catalogue specification of the first production Bonneville was, for Triumph, a most audacious departure from the touring image of the day. It portrayed 'the highest performance standard production motorcycle offered in 1959 with individually bench-tested twin carburettor engines producing 46 bhp at 6500 rpm – a motorcycle for the really knowledgeable enthusiast appreciating the use and power provided'.

Although fitted with deep valanced mudguards, two-level twinseat and traditional Triumph nacelle, it offered a twin splayed inlet port alloy cylinder head and twin 'chopped off' Amal Monobloc carburettors with a remotely rubber-mounted Amal TT float bowl, in conjunction with a previously unheard of combination of racing inlet and sports exhaust camshafts. Also added to this list of ingredients was a Lucas Red Label K2FC Competition manual magneto altogether producing, and often exceeding, the claimed bhp output. The colour scheme was lower half fuel tank and mudguard central stripes in Tangerine (Gold lined) with Pearl Grey mudguards and tank top half.

Although this colour scheme appealed to the home market, the general Export and US recipients pressed for a significant return to the Meriden 'Trade Mark' – Blue. Halfway through the season a change was made to Royal Blue in place of the Tangerine (or Azure Blue as the paint shop cans were labelled and later became known). The only other change was to a wafer-thin Sports twinseat incorporating a Grey lower rim trim band, and reversion to flatter road type handlebars in place of the first downswept 'Sports' versions.

As this machine had the basic engine specification that the US competition boys had hitherto to build up for themselves, the complication of the handsome streamstyled, and very British nacelle was to prove to them to be entirely an unnecessary impediment.

Once again, US pressure resulted in the disappearance of this treasured Triumph emblem, and replacement in 1960 by the chromed sports headlamp assembly. The Amal remotely-mounted TT carburettor float bowl was also proving to be a bit expensive, and unnecessarily fiddly, being originally clamped to the frame seat down tube. So for 1960 a simpler version of float bowl arrangement, using a rubber bush suspended from the engine rear torque steady plate, provided the same overall effect. The Lucas K2FC auto-advance magneto became a K2FC manual. But the major improvement was to build the whole machine into a new lightweight duplex frame with a modified steering head angle to tighten up the steering geometry.

Even before the 1961 season had arrived, this new duplex frame had problems of fracture at the steering headlug, which was overcome by introducing an additional and successfully integral reinforcing tank rail. The first version of the frame produced a smooth, almost vibration free motorcycle, whereas the stiffer replacement version resulted in much harsher characteristics. It appeared that the earlier frame absorbed the inherent cyclic vibration forces and thereby initiated the classic type of premature fatigue failure, whereas the replacement withstood the attack and passed it on to the rider! Other improvements introduced were, for the first time, fully-floating brake shoes, and relocation of the lighting switch on the right side of the machine, below the rider's seat. As one complaining customer put it – 'one has to be a long armed Gibbon with eyes in the finger tips to operate it!'

By 1962 the cracks in the Edward Turner policy of 'I will tell them ... etc etc' were beginning to show. The East and West Coast Distributors could no longer agree between themselves on commonised specifications, and it was from this point model variant proliferation began. So now we had Home & Export T120 models, USA T120R East and West coast models and T120 'C' Competition versions. However, at this stage, this only involved alternative colour schemes, smaller fuel tanks, upswept exhaust systems, wader magnetos and low output stators.

The following season the Bonneville, although still bearing the name, was in fact almost an entirely new motorcycle, yet contained sufficient of the earlier successful motive components to qualify as the next step in the unfolding development of the original theme.

This 1963 model now introduced a further new frame with an immensely stiff single down tube to suit the entirely new and compact unit – construction 650 cc engine, gearbox and transmission unit. This metamophosis cunningly epitomised the philosophy of Triumph development over the previous twenty years and in fact heralded its continuation for the next ten, or more.

Although obviously new, it contained enough of the old to ensure the minimum of disruption to production, but maximum elimination of the older 'hardy-annual' problems. Although the new crankcase looked different, yet familiar, it housed all (or most) of the earlier moving parts, including the gearbox.

Major changes included an engine balance factor alteration to match the new frame, twin coil ignition contact breakers replacing the magneto (this really was a retrograde step — only to be eradicated many years later by the 1979 introduction of electronic ignition), and triplex primary drive and associated components.

Other interesting changes were new front forks incorporating external springs, allowing more internal space to provide additional damping characteristics, a hinged twinseat, and the infamous 'Emergency starting facility in the event of a flat battery'. Almost the wish being father to the event! The paint finish for this year was Alaskan White fuel tank and mudguards for all models and all markets, but this was about all that was commonised.

This year the West Coast Distributor took an additional competition variant, a version of their T120C model, but with all lighting equipment removed and a straight-through exhaust system. This model, although produced straight down the Meriden assembly line, had full twin race camshafts and cam followers, 'chopped-off' Amal Monobloc carburettors with a flexibly mounted remote float bowl, and came complete with 'ready-fix' racing number plate fixing points.

So successful was this 'out-of-the-crate' competition machine, in California in particular, that for the following year (1964) it bore the honoured title 'TT Special', in commemoration of completing as the winner of the 50 lap 'TT' US National Championship in Gardena, California. (The US type TT course of the day was a quarter mile kidney-shaped track on dry clay with an aviating high jump halfway round the course.) 1964 also saw the East Coast only taking the 'Lamped'/upswept silencer competition T120C, but both coasts taking the 'TT' Special — now upgraded from 8.5:1 compression ratio to 11.2:1 with $1\frac{3}{16}$ inch choke Amal Monobloc carburettors and a full energy transfer ignition system. By now the machine had acquired a claimed full 54 bhp at 6500 rpm.

Competition events at home and abroad brought a continuous flow of reported successes, trophies and records, too numerous to list. The AMA Motorcycle World's Speed Record had been 'upped' by diminutive Bill Johnson in September, 1962 to 224.57 mph. in Joe Dudex's Streamliner, with an absolute World's Record Speed (using blended fuel) of 230.669 mph. Neither of these records had been beaten in October, 1964, and in fact the team of Robert Blueflot, Alex Tremulus and Bob Leppan with Gyronaut X-1 continued to break and advance the AMA World's Speed Record to 264.437 mph on the 20th October, 1970, which remaining unbeaten for four years gave Leppan the unique claim to be the World's fastest motorcyclist from 1966 to 1974. The Gyronaut X-1, it must be admitted, had two Bonneville engines in tandem, but nevertheless provided an unbeaten power/weight challenge that stands proudly in the Bonneville record book.

Inevitably and inexorably as progress demands in this motorcycle business, the standard road Bonneville was subsequently fitted with the same cams, followers and carburettors specified for the TT model two years previously, with 9.5 to 1 compression ratio pistons replacing the 8.5s fitted since 1959, and the new twelve volt, Zener diode-controlled electrical system. Yet again a change was made to the frame steering head angle, from 65° to 62° to improve high speed handling characteristics, never a source of complaint by 'Mr Average Guy' on the road — but the current welter of competition and racing successes since the new version of the 'Bonnie' introduced in 1963 had demanded the re-think. But 1967 was to be the last year of that strange but extremely successful variant of the Bonneville, the TT Special. It had run its course, and gained its full honours.

1970 marked the last year of the true Meriden Bonneville, for the 1971 model was to be the long awaited culmination of the Umberslade P39 Project, the new version with oil-in-frame oil reservoir, with entirely new front forks developed by the ex-aircraft industry design teams, and surmounted by the strange flattened rubber-mounted head-lamp suspended on a chromed wire framework. Conical alloy front and rear hubs featured new drum brakes and the introduction of the ugly four gallon slab-sided fuel tank signalled the final end of the Edward Turner egg or teardrop design form.

In 1971, the finish was catalogued as Tiger Gold and Black, rather reminiscent of the camouflage finish of a World War II Tank. Five-speed gearboxes were offered as an alternative on the Bonneville for the first time.

The major change for 1972 was from Black and Gold fuel tanks to White and Gold, with the reluctant but finally inevitable reintroduction of an alternative teardrop-shaped 3 gallon petrol tank for the USA.

However, more of the Umberslade look disappeared in 1973, with the additional introduction of the long awaited 750cc engine, there being not much left to squeeze from the earlier 650cc range. In fact both 650 and 750 models were offered with four or five speed gearboxes in 1973 and 1974, but by far the biggest single improvement was the incorporation of the single front disc brake, and loss of the bent wire headlamp arrangement in favour of the more conventional fork

Super Profile

headlamp mounting pressings, regular headlamp fork gaiters.

Between 1966 and 1967 the Meriden Co-operative had been formed, and production of the Bonneville re-commenced with the notable introduction of left-footshift gear pedal operation and disc brake on the rear. During this time, the 650cc T120 version of the Bonneville was phased out. A limited edition in 1977, to commemorate the Queen's Jubilee, was produced, known simply as the 750cc T140 Bonneville Jubilee Model. It was available in home, overseas and US specifications. On the first of June 1978 the sealed carburettor T140E model appeared specifically to comply with US Federal legislation and was available in Tawny Brown and Gold, Astral Blue and Silver, and Candy Apple and Red, three most attractive colour scheme combinations.

These models continued from 1979, until the 1982 season, with the addition of an Executive model, stylishly equipped with alloy wheels, panniers, luggage boxes, fairing and screen all to match. To this luxury specification was added an electric starter.

1983 models listed the TSX model, and with an entirely new Weslake 8 valve cylinder head fitted, the TSS model, catalogued technically as the T140W-TSS. At the same time the Police Model was being produced from a Bernard Hooper originated design with the 'AV' floating engine designed frame, which also was made available on a small number of Executive models that were produced at the time.

Another very interesting T140 Bonneville derivative that only just saw the light of day was the 650cc Thunderbird, a name rekindled like the Phoenix from the earlier first 1951 650cc model in the Edward Turner design era, from which the Bonneville itself had originally emanated.

But as 1983 approached, mounting liabilities and critical cash flow problems with the inevitable ultimate inability to procure the basic raw materials necessary to ensure continued production, brought manufacture slowly but inexorably to a standstill, despite future orders in hand.

Finally, the Bank appointed a liquidator to wind up the affairs of the Co-operative, and to reduce the outstanding liabilities, an auction of the entire contents and work in progress was held on the last two days of November, and the first of December, 1983.

The buildings, land, projected designs, copyrights, titles, drawings and even the name of Triumph itself had already been disposed of, so that within a couple of months of the auction, almost every vestige of the factory at Meriden, the mecca of post-war Triumph enthusiasts, had been razed to the ground for ever.

But the motorcycle business is a strange blend of loyalty, enthusiasm and commerce. As these words are being written a small but dedicated band of Meriden folk are concentrated in Devon, with a nucleus of both brand new manufacturing machinery and the familiar jigs, tools and fixtures around them, setting about with determination the task of building again the famous Triumph Bonneville.

And somewhere else, in the depths of the Midlands, a 'never really revealed' project, designed originally by the men of Meriden to meet the legislative demands of the next generation of motorcycles, the water-cooled 'Phoenix' twin, is quietly developing and maturing.

All this really does seem to be the stuff of which legends are made.

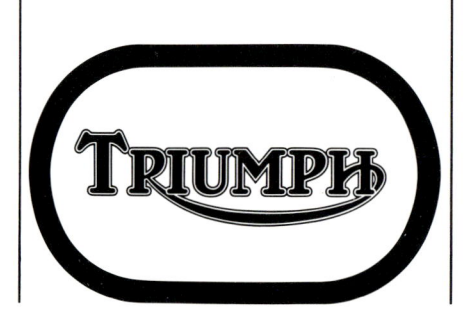

SPECIFICATION

Specifications

Significant engine numbers and change points in the history of the Triumph Bonneville model

1959 models
    First series engine numbers commencing   (4-9-58)   T120   020377
        Additional gearbox adjuster   023111
        Induction hardened camplate   023941

1960 models ('Mouth-organ' tank badges)
    Commencing engine numbers   (10-9-59)   T120   029720
        Duplex frame
        AC generator
        Lucas K2FC (auto) magneto
            Engine series without prefix up to   (28-9-59)   T120   030419
            With 'D' prefix subsequently from   (17-11-59)   T120   D1312
            (Prefix 'D' for duplex frame)

1961 models
    Commencing engine number   (1-9-60)   T120R   D7727
                (15-9-60)   T120C   D8332

        'Reinforced' duplex frame
        Revised steering head angle
        Fully floating brake shoes

1962 models
    Commencing engine number   T120   D15789
        71% engine balance factor
        Needle roller layshaft bearings
        Smiths 140 mph speedometer
        85% balance factor introduced   D17043

1963 models
    Commencing engine number   T120   DU 101
        First unit construction engine model
        Nine stud cylinder barrel
        Crankshaft timing side oil seal
        Twin contact breakers
        $\frac{3}{8}$ in. pitch duplex primary chain
        46T rear sprocket and drum
        Smiths chronometric speedometer and tachometer.
            (Prefix 'DU' signifies unit-construction)

Super Profile

1964 models
    Commencing engine number   T120 DU 5825
        $1\frac{1}{8}$ in. dia choke Amal Monobloc carburettors
        Single unit air filter box
        125 mph magnetic speedometer & matching tachometer
        External front fork springs
        US 'TT' model introduced

1965 models
    Commencing engine number   T120 DU 13375
        Alloy exhaust pipe adaptors in cylinder head

1966 models
    Commencing engine number   T120 DU 24875
        9:1 compression ratio
        Lighter flywheel
        Pressure oil fed cam followers (tappets)
        Revised frame steering head angle (65° – 62°)
        Fairing attachment lugs
        New 8 in. diameter full width hub and brake drum
        Bolt-on rear (46T) sprocket
        Rear wheel speedometer drive box
        12 volt electrics with Zener diode control
        'Birds-wing' tank badges

1967 models
    Commencing engine number   T120 DU 44394
        Twin pancake air filters
        150 mph speedometer
        Amal 389 Type Monobloc carburettors   DU 52578
        Lucas encapsulated alternator stator   DU 58565
        Timed (pressure fed) cam followers (tappets)   DU 63241

1968 models
    Commencing engine number   T120 DU 66246
        12 point cylinder base nuts
        Lucas 6CA contact breakers
        Twin L.S. 8 in. diameter front brake Full width hub with air scoop
        'Finned-egg' Zener Diode heat sink
        Stroboscope rotor/ignition timing pointer   DU 83021

1969 models
    Commencing engine number   T120 DU 85904
        Heavier flywheel
        New connecting rods
        Stronger piston crowns
        L/H threaded tachometer drive gearbox
        Square 'picture-frame' tank badges
        Coupled exhaust system (balance pipe)
        Lucas RM21 stator
        Twinseat passenger guard rail

        Nitrided camshafts   DU 87105
        Anti-theft engine number raised pads   DU 86965
        Termination of original Triumph numbering system   DU 90282
        Introduction of revised USA numbering system   JC 00101
        Wider front forks ($6\frac{1}{2}$ in – $6\frac{3}{4}$ in.) centres   AC 10464

1970 models
    Commencing engine number   T120   JD 24894
        Deletion of engine timed (camshaft) breather
        Carburettor bowls incorporating plastic drain plugs
        'Bolt-on' front engine plates
        Leaf-spring gearbox indexing   ED 32044

1971 models
    Commencing engine number   (18-10-70)   T120   NE 01436
        First series "Umberslade" Bonnie
        'Slab-sided' 4 gallon fuel tank
        Duplex frame with 4 pints oil capacity
        Metric timing side main bearing   GE 27209

1972 models
    Commencing engine number   (6-7-71)   T120   HG 30882
        Push-in exhaust pipes
        Bolt-on inlet port adaptors
        Rocker boxes with (4 screw) finned inspection covers
        5 speed gearbox on 'V' models
        Lowered frame

1973 models
    Commencing engine number   (18-8-72)   T120V JH 15366
        T410 model introduced
            initially as 75 x 82 mm   (22-9-72)   T140V KH 17124
                                            up to   T140V XH 22018
            then as 76 x 82 mm   (14-12-72)   T140V XH 22019
        T120 model continues — all with:-
        $\frac{3}{8}$ in. pitch triplex primary chain
        Rubber fork gaiters
        Chromed headlamp brackets
        Front disc brake
        'Slim-line' silencers (curved end-cones)
        New-type tachometer drive gearbox   (19-1-73)   AH 23894
        Revised pistons (71-3676) fitted   (13-2-73)   BH 25987
        6 screw rocker covers   (1-3-73)   CH 26775
As from 17 July 1973 Triumph Engineering Company Limited
became a subsidiary of N.V.T. Limited

1974 models
    Commencing engine number (1973 model in 1974 colours)   T140V GJ 55101
        First full specification 1974 model   (30-8-73)   JJ 58013
        Steering damper deleted
        New silencers with tapered end cones
Last model built by T.E.C. and sold by N.V.T   (16-10-73)   T140V NJ 60061
                                                                              T120V NJ 60070

1975 models
    Commencing engine number   T140V DK 61000
        First models assembled by Meriden Motorcycles — from
        existing previous stocks of material up to:-
        Last R.H. gearshift   (7-4-75)   T140V GK 62243

1976 models
    Commencing engine number   (10-7-75)   T140V HN 62501
        First model of Meriden Cp-operatives own manufacture
        L.H. footshift gearchange
        Rear wheel disc brake

Super Profile

1977 models
    Commencing engine number   T140V GP 73000
        Introduction of Jubilee Model   GP 81000

1978 models
    Commencing engine number   T140V HX 00100
        Introduction of 'E' Model   T140E BX 04570
        Veglia instruments
        Yuasa battery
        Halogen headlamp

1979 models
    Commencing engine number   T140E HA 11001
        Electronic ignition
        3 phase alternator
        New handlebar switches
        Neutral indicator
        New instruments and panel
        Gas rear shock absorber units
        Amal MkII carburettor – standard
        Lockable twinseat

    Introduction of T140 'D' Model 'Special' in all-black
    gold-lined finish and Lester alloy wheels   (14-2-78)   T140D XA 16355

1980 models
    Commencing engine number   (5-11-79)   T140V PB 25001
        Rear brake caliper now above wheel centreline

1981 models
    Commencing engine number   T140V KDA 28001
        T140ES model with electric starter
        Re-introduction of exhaust-stubs in cylinder head
        Morris alloy wheels replace Lester

1982 models
    Commencing engine number   (5-5-81)   T140V EDA 30001
        AV model introduced for police use
        TR7T Trophy Trail now in catalogue
        TR65 Thunderbird announced

1983 models
    Commencing engine number   (15-2-82)   T140V BEA 33001
        TSS model with 8 valve Weslake cylinder head,
        new crankshaft with $1\frac{7}{8}$ in. big end journals and
        wide crank webs, alloy cylinder, central spark plug,
        34 mm. C.V. carbs and twin front disc option.
        TSX model with low-rider styling and cast alloy wheels
        with twin front disc option
        TR65T Thunderbird
        TR6T Tiger Trail (to order only as A 650cc model)
        T140E model
        The above models continue to the closure of Meriden,
        and the final end of the Co-operative
        Last machine produced   (21-1-83)   T140V AEA 34393

Super Profile

	1959	1960/1/2	1963-70	1971	1974	1975-83	
Bore & Stroke (mm)	71 x 82	71 x 82	71 x 82	71 x 82	76 x 82	76 x 82	‡Intermediate 1971 724cc version (75 x 82)
Cubic capacity (cc)	649	649	649	649	744	744	
Compression ratio	8.5	8.5	‡8.5	9	7.9	7.9	‡T120 9:1 from 1966
BHP @ R.P.M.	46 @ 6500	46 @ 6500	‡46 @ 6500	47 @ 6700	@ 7000	@ 7000	‡47 @ 6700 from 1965
Gear ratios (overall)							*1961/2 1973 & 4
1st	11.2	*11.38	11.84	12.10	‡12.78	12.25	11.92 12.25
2nd	7.75	7.88	8.17	8.36	9.10	8.63	8.25 8.63
3rd	5.45	5.55	5.76	6.15	6.92	6.58	5.81 6.58
4th	4.57	4.66	4.88	4.95	5.89	5.59	4.88 5.59
5th	—	—	—	—	4.95	4.70	— 4.70
Sprocket sizes							
Engine	24	‡22	29	29	29	29	‡1961/2 21T
Clutch	43	43	58	58	58	58	
Final drive	18	18	19	19	*19	20	20T from 1973
Rear wheel	46	43	46	47	47	47	
Front suspension							
Spring	Internal	Internal	‡Internal	External	External	External	‡External from 1964 @ 30 lb/in and 26½ lb/in from 1965
Rate (lb/in)	Red	Blk/White	32	25	25	25	
Rear suspension							
Oil/Gas	Oil	Oil	Oil	Oil	Oil	‡Oil	‡Gas shocks from 1978
Spring rate (lb/in)	100	‡100	145	*110	*110	100	‡145 from 1962 * 100 from 1972
Wheel/tyre sizes							
Front	3.25x19	3.25x19	‡3.25x19	3.25x19	3.25x19	*3.25x19	‡3.00x19 1967 on – *4.10x19 from 1979
Rear	3.50x19	‡3.50x19	3.50x18	4.00x18	4.00x18	*4.00x18	‡4.00x18 1961 on – *4.10x18 from 1979
Chains							
Primary (Pilch-width-links)	½x0.305x70	½x0.305x70	⅜ Duplex x 84	‡⅜ Duplex x 84	⅜ Triplex x 84	⅜ Triplex x 84	‡⅜ Triplex x 84 from 1973
Rear	⅝x⅜x101	⅝x⅜x98	‡⅝x⅜x103	⅝x⅜x106	⅝x⅜x106	⅝x⅜x106	‡104 links from 1967
Capacities (Imp)							
Fuel tank – gals	4	4	4	4	4	4	
Oil tank (reservoir) pts	5	5	‡5	4	4	5	‡1970 5½ pts (imp)
Gearbox – pts (cc)	⅔(400)	⅔(400)	⅞(500)	⅞(500)	⅞(500)	⅞(500)	
Primary case	¼(150)	¼(150)	⅝(350)	‡¼(150)	¼(150)	¼(150)	‡Initial fill only
Front forks (cc each leg)	1/6 (100)	¼(150)	‡¼(150)	⅓(190)	⅓(190)	⅓(190)	‡⅓(190 cc) from 1964
Electrical Eqpt –							
Generator type	E3L Dyno						
Battery	6v	6v	‡6v	12v	12v	12v	‡12v introduced in 1966
Contact breaker	Magneto	magneto	‡4CA	*6CA	*6CA	□6CA	‡6CA in 1968 * 10CA in 1973 □ Electronic in 1979
Ignition timing (BTC)	7/16 in	7/16 in	‡39°	38°	38°	38°	‡38° in 1970
Dimensions							
Wheelbase (ins)	55¾	54½	*55	56	56	56	*55½ from 1967
Ground clearance (ins)	5	5	5	7½	7	7	
Seat height (ins)	30½	30½	30½	32	33	31	
Width (ins)	28½	28½	27	33	33	*33	*29 from 1980
Dry weight (lbs)	404	393	*363	382	395	‡395	*390 lb from 1969 ‡418 Electric start

17

Super Profile

THE MOTOR CYCLE, 1 DECEMBER 1960

ROAD IMPRESSIONS OF NEW MODELS

649 c.c. Triumph Bonneville 120

SPARKLING PERFORMANCE FROM THE LATEST VERSION OF A FAMOUS ROADBURNER

TRACTABLE POWER, SUPERB BRAKES AND GOOD ROADHOLDING *By DAVID DIXON*

I AM much too well bred ever to give the raspberry. But to those who chant that 100 m.p.h. motor cycles are noisy and intractable I give the nearest (well-bred) approach to the raspberry I can muster. My views on the subject have been mightily reinforced after a few days, mainly very wet days, spent on a 1961 Triumph Bonneville 120.

The era when performance at the top end of the scale was achieved to the detriment of poke at the other end is decidedly past. This mile-eater will span 80 m.p.h.—from 25 to 105 m.p.h.—in top gear. And what's more it achieves that nigh-incredible feat without fuss or coaxing. In weather more favourable than I had, that 105 m.p.h. figure, by the way, could be very handsomely bettered.

It was just my luck that such an exciting beastie should come along when rain, rain, rain, was the order of the week. More than my enthusiasm was in for a damping—or so I thought as I threw a leg over the Bonneville for the first time. But the model was as impatient as I to reach the wide open spaces, even if the roads were under water.

The Bonneville, it is true, will tick-tock along at 30 m.p.h. with the top cog in mesh, but this is no town runabout. As soon as the speed-limit signs are left behind, you drop down a ratio, or maybe two, and get to work on the right grip. Characteristically Triumph, power is on tap from the moment the grip is tweaked. There is no hesitancy, no fluffing. Those twin carburettors really do their stuff.

In bottom gear, in an almost alarmingly short time, the Bonneville will reach 50

© Iliffe Specialist Publications Ltd., 1960

m.p.h. A quick upward flick on the gear pedal and 70 m.p.h. shows. As third is snicked home there comes another beefy surge, 88-90 m.p.h. comes up and things begin to get exciting. Then top is engaged.

Wind pressure on a bulky, riding-coated, overtrousered and booted figure slows the rapid, forward tramp in the 94-95 m.p.h. region. A semi-crouch excites the speedometer again and the needle will teeter readily round the 105 m.p.h. mark.

On a dry, deserted road, with a two-piece-suited rider adopting a racing crouch, my guess is that it would be rela-

tively cushy to beat 110 or even 115 m.p.h. I am writing, incidentally, in terms of *indicated* speeds. There was no real opportunity to test the clock for accuracy. But I had no reason to believe it unduly optimistic.

Maximum speeds of the order of 110 m.p.h. are, of course, of little more than academic interest. A high, genuinely usable, cruising speed is of far more importance. Right then. Settle for 85 m.p.h.? That's chicken feed for this baby. Wherever road conditions permit, speeds of that order can be maintained without fuss. Farther up the scale a high-

Below left: The engine remained oiltight throughout. The folding kick-starter pedal rotates and the light switch is located beneath the seat. Right: Two Amal Monobloc carburettors are fitted as standard

The Motor Cycle, 1 December 1960

frequency tremor at the handlebar can be felt—a tremor that is present also at equivalent engine speeds in the indirect ratios. It disappears at 100 m.p.h.

So the machine is a flyer. What is sacrificed for performance? Tractability? Not a bit. Pulling away from a standstill can be accomplished as readily on the 8.25 to 1 second gear as in the 11.92 to 1 bottom ratio. Noise? The most grumpy of grumpy silence-please addicts couldn't complain of that.

The performance, then, is fully usable without objection. True, there is some mechanical noise from the valve gear but that wouldn't trouble anyone but the most fastidious perfectionist. Thirst? Overall fuel consumption was about 52 m.p.g.

Those twin carburettors needed careful synchronization for slow idling, but, at best, idling was not always completely reliable. Another mild snag with twin carburettors is that twistgrip operation is somewhat heavier than it is with a single instrument. But these are minor debits in such a glowing balance sheet.

Provided the carburettors were flooded, first-prod starting was the rule even after the model had spent a night in the November open. Quite a bit of muscle is required, by the way, to bump the engine over compression—the ratio is 8.5 to 1.

To stifle any tendency toward pinking, 100-octane petrol was used throughout. I ran out of fuel on one occasion. Believe it or not, this magnificent motor cycle has no reserve tap.

The gear box lived fully up to the Triumph reputation. Pedal movement is up for upward changes and down for down. Gear selection is rapid and noiseless, though, between second and third, a slight pause in pedal travel is essential. The new clutch friction material employed effectively eliminates sticking plates. There is no longer any need even to free the plates before the first start of the day. Provided the engine was idling slowly, bottom gear could be noiselessly engaged. Pleasantly light in operation, the clutch took up the drive smoothly and without snatch.

For assessing roadholding and handling I could hardly have chosen worse conditions. On one 400-mile run I had only some 50 miles of dry road. It is all the more credit to the model, then, that I at no time had the least cause for anxiety. Yet *average* speeds most of the time were in the mid-fifties.

Steering is considerably heavier than that of previous Triumphs, and considerably improved by being more positive. Torsionally, the duplex frame is extremely rigid. The model is rock-steady at all speeds. There are few machines I would ride hands-off at 80-plus on wet, windy days and on greasy roads, but I had no qualms about doing so with the Bonneville.

Some slight effort was required to lay the machine into a corner; but once on line, it stayed there. In typical Triumph fashion the machine could be heeled well over until something grounded—the prop stand on the left or the footrest on the right.

Roundabouts were great fun and sinuous West Country roads even more so. In spite of its appearance, the Bonneville is not in the least top-heavy. It can be chucked around with all the abandon of an expert juggler pitching Indian clubs.

I would have preferred softer suspension. The spring poundage could with advantage be reduced. Both front and rear forks are well damped, although that up front is very sensitive to changes of temperature.

Initially, I thought the riding position rather cramped. But, after several hours of high-speed blasting, I had a complete change of heart. It is just right for the job. Reasonably short and flat, the handlebar gives just the right degree of forward lean for counteracting wind pressure. And the rear of the three-gallon tank is narrow, affording excellent knee grip.

On any high-speed roadster, powerful braking is of vital importance. A Triumph modification for 1961 allows the shoes to float, and the linings are resited round towards the trailing ends of the shoes. The result is impressive to say the least.

Cheeks creased by wind pressure, David Dixon and the Bonneville crack along at 80-plus near Runnymede. Below: The new front brake in its full-width hub incorporates floating shoes and improved lining location

Light in operation, both brakes were extremely powerful and—an excellent feature—they were unaffected by water.

The chromium-plated headlamp takes one back to the days of pre-war Triumphs. There is no nacelle—and, as on the Trophy models, the headlamp unit is quickly detachable; the wiring harness is connected to a quick-release multi-pin plug behind the lamp. Adequate power

19

Super Profile

THE MOTOR CYCLE, 1 DECEMBER 1960

for 60-65 m.p.h. cruising was provided by the headlamp beam. The light switch is located beneath the dual-seat (with the best of intentions, no doubt), but how are you supposed to reach it when you are on the move? Giving a quick flash from pilot to main beam for overtaking is impossible. No marks for that one.

I liked the sporty appearance of the narrow mudguards but they are hardly suitable for wet-weather riding. Another detail criticism is that the steering-damper knob repeatedly unscrewed. My only other point concerns the oil filler cap; when can we have one that doesn't seep oil?

Outweighing these criticisms by a long chalk are detail features to appeal to any enthusiast. The control cables, for example, have cam adjusters at the handlebar ends. That roll-on centre stand really does its stuff. Twistgrip friction is easily adjusted by means of a spring-loaded screw with knurled knob. The throttle-cable adjuster is readily accessible.

That, then, is the Bonneville 120 as I found it. It is a machine that is very, very fast, and, with its excellent handling and superb brakes, safe to ride almost irrespective of the conditions. It may not be quite so tractable as some, but there is nothing about its power and torque characteristics to render it in the least unsuitable for town work. In fact, in any company, this latest Bonneville is an absolute honey, with no vices—and attributes by the score.

Above: Built primarily for the purpose of defeating time, the Bonneville is acceptably orthodox in appearance

Left: The flat handlebar aids high-speed motoring and the ball-end control levers are there to comply with competition requirements. The tank top grid saves the paintwork when carrying luggage

Old and new. The Bonneville may not be built like Windsor Castle but it enhances the entrance setting

SPECIFICATION

ENGINE: Triumph 649 c.c. (71 x 82mm). overhead-valve parallel twin; plain big-end bearings; crankshaft supported in two ball bearings. Light-alloy cylinder head; cast-iron cylinder block; compression ratio, 8.5 to 1.

CARBURETTORS: Two Amal Monobloc; no air slides.

ELECTRICAL EQUIPMENT: Lucas RM 13/15 alternator charging 6-volt, 12-ampere-hour battery through rectifier. Quickly detachable Lucas 7in-diameter pre-focus headlamp with 30/24-watt main bulb and integral pilot light. Lucas magneto ignition with auto-advance.

TRANSMISSION: Triumph four-speed gear box driven by ½ x 0.305in chain through multi-plate clutch with bonded friction faces. Gear ratios: top, 4.88 to 1; third, 5.81 to 1; second, 8.25 to 1; bottom, 11.92 to 1. Final drive by ⅜ x ⅜in chain.

SUSPENSION: Triumph telescopic front fork with two-way hydraulic damping. Pivoted rear fork controlled by adjustable Girling spring units incorporating hydraulic damping.

TYRES: Dunlop 3.25 x 19in ribbed front and 4.00 x 18in Universal rear.

BRAKES: 8in-diameter front; 7in-diameter rear.

FUEL CAPACITY: 3 gallons.

OIL CAPACITY: 5 pints.

DIMENSIONS: Wheelbase, 56½in; ground clearance, 5in unladen; seat height, 31in; weight, 403 lb with about one gallon of petrol and full oil tank.

PRICE: £288 5s 11d (including £49 5s 11d British purchase tax). Extras: Quickly detachable rear wheel, £3 16s; prop stand, 19s 11d; pillion footrests, 19s 11d; steering lock, 13s 3d.

MANUFACTURERS: Triumph Engineering Co., Ltd., Meriden Works, Allesley, Coventry.

Printed in England by Cornwall Press Ltd., Paris Garden, London. S.E.1. RP11365—N111

MOTOR CYCLE 2 FEBRUARY 1967

649 cc TRIUMPH BONNEVILLE
ROAD TESTS OF NEW MODELS

Power-packed Bonnie attractively finished in purple and white

Some 48 bhp at a modest 6,800 rpm are churned out by this six-fifty power plant

HOW often can you use a bike's top speed? Never, if you stay within the speed limits in over-regulated Britain.

But how many times is full-hole *acceleration* feasible? That's a different matter. A solo which can out-rocket almost all other vehicles is not merely a useful bike but an exciting one. Such is the Triumph Bonneville. Moreover, what the latest Bonnie gives is just about the most sophisticated behaviour you could wish for in a sporting mount.

A standing-start quarter-mile in 14.3s is shattering enough, but the way the model behaves has to be sampled to be appreciated. Tractable power is on tap from the 1,200-rpm tickover right up the scale to the peak-power figure of 6,800 rpm. At any point there is an effortless flow of zestful acceleration available, as befits a thoroughbred from the factory that pioneered the vertical twin.

MOTOR CYCLE 2 FEBRUARY 1967

the handlebar and footrests; above 5,000 rpm (80 mph in top gear) it was felt almost entirely through the seat.

No carburettor air slides are fitted yet, with each carburettor lightly flooded, the engine invariably responded to the first or second kick following a cold, but not frosty, night in the open.

Within a minute or two of a cold start the engine settled down to an even, reliable tickover. Some mechanical clatter came from the valve gear but was lost on the wind once the bike was under way.

Just off the pilot jet was a flat spot in the carburation which occasionally caused the engine to stall. The fault could not be cured by adjusting the air screw and was most often encountered after throttling back to the slowest possible tickover for noiseless engagement of bottom gear.

Moderately heavy in operation but sweet in take-up, the clutch stood up magnificently to innumerable full-throttle standing-starts when the performance figures were logged. No adjustment was necessary during the test.

Upward gear changes called for an unhurried two-stage movement of the pedal if a noiseless swop was to be achieved. Downward changes required a precisely synchronized blip of the twistgrip.

Recent frame improvements have endowed the Bonneville with steering and roadholding on a par with virtually any comparable road-burner.

Changing from a 3.25 × 18in front tyre to one of 3.00 × 19in has resulted in more precise steering without any lack of adhesion in slippery conditions. Steering is light, especially as the 100-mph mark is approached.

When the top-speed figures were clocked there was a suspicion of weaving which was lessened but not eliminated by a turn or two on the steering-damper knob.

Through sharp S-bends, the Bonneville could be cranked from left to right easily and

On the open road a tweak of the grip sends the speed surging up to the 70-mph limit. Exhaust silencing is effective enough to allow such performance to be used without offending bystanders.

With power so widespread, change-up speeds are relatively uncritical. However, upward changes are probably best made at 5,000 rpm (32, 54 and 66 mph), 1,800 rpm below peak-power revs.

Gearing is on the lowish side and at top speed with the rider in a racing crouch the engine is over-buzzing in top gear.

In the soft rubber mountings for the handlebar, revmeter-and-speedometer assembly and the petrol tank there is tacit acknowledgment that vibration is characteristic of production vertical twins.

However, the latest Bonneville is almost certainly the smoothest of the line: only between 4,400 and 5,000 rpm could vibration be felt through

Above left: Proving the roadholding in adverse conditions. Above right: Twin Amal carbs, each on its own inlet stub

Functional control layout. Tank-top luggage grid is standard

22

MOTOR CYCLE 2 FEBRUARY 1967

without fear of grounding anything at extreme cornering angles.

For threading dense traffic and turning round in narrow roads, more steering lock would have been welcome.

At low speeds the soft, long action of the front fork absorbed practically all surface irregularities, yet on fast, bumpy bends there was no pitching. Firmer in action, the rear suspension struts were well damped on recoil and effectively swallowed shocks at high and low speeds.

So smooth and controllable were the brakes that they gave little hint of their power until applied really hard; hence the excellent stopping distance of 29ft from 30 mph came as a surprise.

With high footrests and lower-than-usual seat, the riding position was compact and required getting accustomed to. However, it proved comfortable on long runs.

Positioned well to the rear, the footrests relieved the legs and arms of the strain of resisting wind pressure at high speeds. At MIRA, incidentally, 100 mph was achieved with the rider sitting up.

The transverse ribs on the dualseat were appreciated, for they prevent the rider from sliding back and forth under hard acceleration and braking.

Positioning of the control pedals was convenient, but a shorter reach to the front-brake and clutch levers would be an improvement.

Above: Handling is improved by the latest smaller-section, bigger-diameter front tyre. Front fork action matches the rear-suspension characteristics

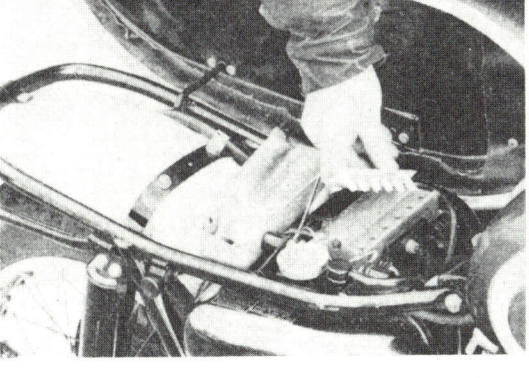

Right: Located under the lift-up dualseat, the battery is easy to top up

Smart and powerful, the Bonneville is a machine the enthusiast is proud to own

Above: The petrol tank is cut away to accommodate the twin ignition coils.

Super Profile

MOTOR CYCLE 2 FEBRUARY 1967

So, too, would thinner hand grips—the fat plastic grips fitted were not entirely comfortable.

Now sited in the headlamp shell, the light switch is partially obscured by the revmeter-speedometer assembly. The ignition and main-beam warning lights, also sited in the back of the headlamp, are completely obscured.

Comfortable after-dark cruising speed on unlit roads was no more than 55 to 60 mph. The headlamp threw a wide pool of light rather than a long beam, which would be preferable.

Routine maintenance tasks were straightforward and the tool roll adequate. A bleed off the engine oil supply goes to the rear chain but the setting was so critical that the chain was either swamped or bone dry.

Throughout the test, the power unit remained completely oiltight and the tank required no topping-up.

Finish is aubergine and white: aubergine is a deep purple and very smart, too.

Detail features to appeal to the enthusiast are finger-operated cable adjusters on the front-brake and clutch levers, an ignition cut-out button by the twistgrip (the ignition switch is under the rider's left thigh), a five-amp lighting fuse under the seat, a steering lock and a petrol tap in each side of the tank, so that a reserve supply can be trapped.

With its blend of sophistication and high performance, the Bonneville cannot but charm even the most discerning enthusiast. It's that sort of machine.

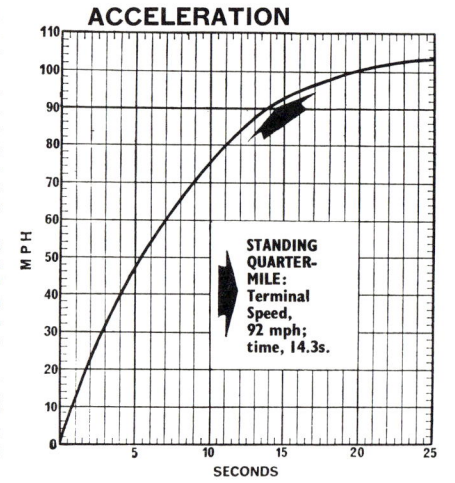

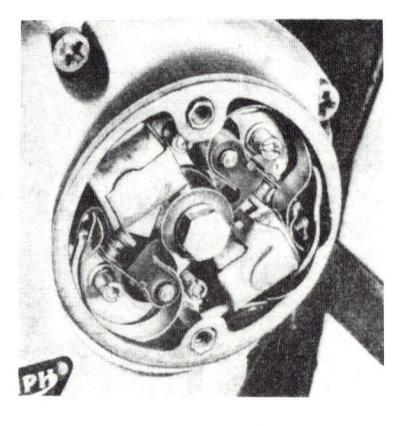

Above right: Twin contact breakers neatly mounted in the timing chest

ACCELERATION

STANDING QUARTER-MILE: Terminal Speed, 92 mph; time, 14.3s.

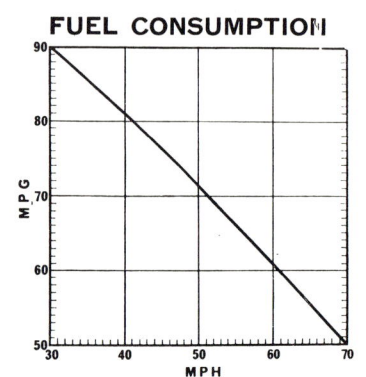

FUEL CONSUMPTION

Bottom-, second- and third-gear figures represent maximum-power revs, 6,800

BOTTOM SECOND THIRD TOP

Motor Cycle ROAD TEST
TRIUMPH BONNEVILLE

SPECIFICATION

ENGINE
Capacity and type: 649 cc (71 × 82mm) overhead-valve parallel twin.
Bearings: Roller drive-side and ball timing-side mains; plain big-ends.
Lubrication: Dry sump; tank capacity 6 pints.
Compression ratio: 9 to 1.
Carburettors: Two Amal Monoblocs. No air filters or cold-start slides.
Claimed output: 48 bhp at 6,800 rpm.

TRANSMISSION
Primary: ⅜in duplex chain in oilbath case.
Secondary: ⅝ × ⅜in chain.
Clutch: Multi-plate.
Gear ratios: 11·81, 8·17, 5·76, 4·84 to 1.
Engine rpm at 30 mph in top gear, 1,950.

ELECTRICAL EQUIPMENT
Ignition: Battery and twin coils.
Charging: Lucas 100-watt alternator to 12-volt, ten-amp-hour battery through rectifier.
Headlamp: 7in-diameter with 50/40-watt main bulb.

FUEL CAPACITY: 4 gallons.

TYRES: Dunlop 3.00 × 19in ribbed front, 3.50 × 18in studded rear.

BRAKES: 8in diameter front and 7in diameter rear, both with floating shoes; finger adjusters.

SUSPENSION: Triumph telescopic front fork with hydraulic damping. Pivoted rear fork controlled by Girling spring-and-hydraulic units; three-position adjustment for load.
DIMENSIONS: Wheelbase, 56in; ground clearance, 5in; seat height 30½in. All unladen.
WEIGHT: 395 lb, including one gallon of petrol.
PRICE: £355 0s 10d including British purchase tax.
EXTRAS: Quickly detachable rear wheel, £5 5s 5d; prop stand, £1 9s 3d; pillion footrests, £1 7s 11d; revmeter assembly, £9 3s 2d.
ROAD TAX: £8 a year; £2 19s for four months.
MAKERS: Triumph Engineering Co, Ltd, Meriden Works, Allesley, Coventry, Warwicks.

PERFORMANCE

(Obtained at the Motor Industry Research Association's proving ground, Lindley, Leicestershire).
MEAN MAXIMUM SPEED: 108 mph (12½-stone rider wearing racing leathers and boots; light side wind).
HIGHEST ONE-WAY SPEED: 110 mph.
BRAKING: From 30 mph to rest on dry tarmac, 29ft.
TURNING CIRCLE: 20ft.
MINIMUM NON-SNATCH SPEED: 20 mph in top gear.
WEIGHT PER CC: 0·61 lb.

Super Profile

OWNER'S VIEW

My first interview was with Steve Whitcombe, of Glastonbury, Somerset, the owner of a 1979 T140E model which he bought new. An accident caused him to change the frame, a task which he found relatively easy, and he has also modified the riding position by fitting clip-ons and and rear-sets, which are better suited to his requirements. His comments are as follows:

JRN. Why are you so interested in the Bonneville?
SW. It is hard to put a finger on any one point about the Bonneville. Good looks, handling, good brakes and fuel consumption come immediately to mind, but if I were to commit myself I would have to say that for me it is the character of the machine.
JRN. When and why did you buy your Bonnie?
SW. I bought my Bonnie, a T140E, in December 1979. Before that I was a Jap biker, until a mate of mine bought a Norton Commando 750 as a box of bits. When he had rebuilt it and given me a ride, I knew I was converted to the ownership of a British bike. I wanted a brand new machine, so the Bonneville was a natural choice. Four and a half years later on, I have no regrets.

JRN. What condition was it in? If you found faults, were these common problems?
SW. I have heard some criticism from other owners about the Mark 2 Concentric carburettors. I find them easy to balance, but some days my Bonnie will tick over, some days not. Also, the standard choke lever arrangement left much to be desired, so I've since converted it to cable-operated choke. The indicators were sometimes tricky to operate, but these, along with the engine 'kill' switch, were long ago removed on my machine. The only real headache I have had is a complete loss of oil pressure on three separate occasions, each just after engine oil changes. Dislodged dirt would find its way into the oil pump ball valves, preventing them from seating. Charlie's, of Bristol, market a sump filter which should prevent this from happening, so I shall get around to buying and fitting one. Another minor irritation is the push-fit exhaust pipes, which for ever leak. The distinctive clicking noise heard when the engine is running sounds like a loose tappet.
JRN. What repair/renovation work has been done, and what advice would you give to someone facing the same problem.
SW. I had to rebuild my Bonnie from a new frame upwards after an accident. This task is made a lot easier with the aid of a genuine parts book. The Bonnie is a really good basic machine to build and I was surprised how easily it went together. That was at 14,000 miles. At 21,000 miles I fitted new piston rings, valves and guides, at 25,000 a new speedometer drive gearbox, and at 30,000 miles new swinging arm bushes. The engine required a new triplex chain at 31,000 miles. About three years ago, I decided I required a better riding position, as the standard Bonnie has the footrests too far forward and the handlebars were not very comfortable at speeds over 70mph. So I fitted clip-ons and rear-sets, which took a while to get used to, but proved worth while in the end. Even with standard handlebars re-fitted, the rear-sets are still comfortable. The cycle parts have always been kept in good condition by applying WD 40, although eventually the lacquer applied to the rear lamp holder and the wheel hubs deteriorates.
JRN. If purchased new, what warranty work was required to bring the machine up to standard, and was it then satisfactory?
SW. The only warranty work I had done was a carburettor adjustment and a rear bulb replaced after the original had vibrated out.
JRN. Have you experienced difficulty in obtaining parts? What solutions, if any, did you find?
SW. I have not had difficulty in obtaining parts; I get all my needs from Charlie's of Bristol. One modification I have made on my machine is to replace the manifold inlet rubbers with small lengths of car radiator hose. But it is necessary first to treat the inside with a fuel-resisting coating, otherwise the rubber will perish and block the inlet tract. The radiator hose lasts much longer than the original rubbers, is cheaper, and doesn't crack. Another useful tip is to carry a spare throttle and clutch cable, both of which can be coiled within the headlamp shell.
JRN. What kind of handling and performance does your machine provide?
SW. Handling is very good with Avon F2 and R2 Roadrunner tyres. The performance is still enough to frighten me. One of the first things I did was to fit Anglo megaphone silencers, which provide a marked increase in acceleration and make a lovely 'gurgling crackle' on the over-run! The gearbox is very positive, but neutral has to be selected just before coming to a halt. The ratios are a little too close together for my liking.
JRN. Is the bike on continual use? How practical is it — are the running costs high?
SW. I use my Bonnie every day and find the further you go, the better it

Super Profile

runs. Fuel consumption works out at around 65mpg with give and take riding. A rear tyre lasts an average of 9,000 miles, but with regard to the front tyre I found it was wearing mainly on the right-hand side due, I believe, to the camber of the roads. Although it still had plenty of tread down the middle, a handling problem developed whereby the handlebars began to oscillate. This was cured when I fitted a new front tyre. The machine does not use much oil and there are no major oil leaks — just a couple of minor ones!

JRN. How helpful is it to be a member of the Triumph owners MCC?

SW. I joined the TOMCC shortly after buying my Bonnie. There is a wealth of information available from members, especially as the most common model is the oil-in-frame T140. Every machine is different and you can get good contacts for spares and special items not normally advertised.

JRN. Is there a specialist you have found particularly helpful?

SW. Charlie's of Bristol for spares and service, Anglo Bike of Beenham for performance 'goodies'.

JRN. How much enjoyment do you get from your machine?

SW. Stacks! I can't stay off it. It always starts and always gets me home. It turns heads and always attracts attention. When I first bought it, people would come up to me and say 'I didn't realise they still made these!'

JRN. What advice would you give to potential Bonneville owners?

SW. Go for it! I never get fed up with mine. It may not be as fast as some Jap bikes, but it must be one of the safest big bikes around today. Get one with electronic ignition and you are laughing. When I bought mine, I ran it in religiously and carried out all the oil changes at regular intervals. 32,000 miles later the engine is somewhat looser, but the bottom end shows no signs of wear. One point to watch out for is the place at which the carburettors enter the air box assembly. Make sure the sealing rings around the carburettor intakes are in good order, otherwise they may get sucked in and jam the throttle wide open, as once happened to me.

My next contact was with Dave Forty, of Harrow, Middlesex, who has another 1979 T140 model, which he bought second-hand, with only 150 miles on the speedometer. Though somewhat more brief, his comments are as follows:

JRN. Why are you so interested in the Bonneville?

DF. I have found it to be a practical means of transport, as well as fun to ride.

JRN. When and why did you buy your Bonnie?

DF. I bought it in December 1980, when I was looking for a bike after having passed my test. The Triumph was one year old and had only 150 miles on the speedometer, yet was being sold for a very reasonable price.

JRN. What condition was it in? If you found faults, were these common problems?

DF. Having spent a year standing, the exhaust pipes and suspension springs had rusted, and the alloy had dulled. The exhaust pipes were renewed, and the rest polished. I replaced the Lucas tungsten filament headlamp with a Cibie Z beam halogen unit.

JRN. What repairs/renovation work has been done, and what advice would you give to anyone facing the same problems?

DF. In the four years I have had my machine, it has done 39,000 miles, and the parts that have needed to be replaced were the sprockets and chains. I have found that the gearbox sprocket seems to last for about 18,000 miles, and I renew chains at 6,000 miles. Rear tyres last for about 12,000 miles. The engine needed a rebore at 32,000 miles, and the valves and guides were changed at 12,000 miles so that the new-type inlets could be fitted to help reduce oil consumption. They were fitted with seals. They were again changed at the time of the rebore, but when one of the exhaust valve guides broke after only a further 7,000 miles, another cylinder head job became necessary. The guide had fractured around the collar and also split along its length. The bits are still in the silencer!

Changing the gearbox sprocket resulted in an oil leak, which took months to fix. The large nut on the high gear pinion needs to be tight in order to compress the 'O' ring under the tab washer, but the thread on the pinion sleeve was undersize such that the nut could not be tightened. A new nut did not help, either. In addition, there was not a chamfer on the collar of the sprocket, in the area where the 'O' ring makes its seal. The answer was to fit yet another sprocket, of the original specification. Another fault can be attributed to the size of the oil seal that goes into the gearbox. Some of the samples supplied are smaller in diameter than others, with the result that oil will leak around the periphery, as well as from the sprocket joint. The answer in this case is to fit an oil seal with the original part number moulded into the rubber.

The black Lucas switches are often a problem, and the indicators on my machine never worked for long, even when a replacement switch was fitted. They were changed for the old 'winged' type, which are also cheaper. I also needed to change the master cylinder on the handlebars, for the front disc brake. A Norton component was used, which had the advantage of being cheaper too. The centre stand broke, was repaired by welding, then broke again. One exhaust pipe fractured and had to be renewed.

JRN. Although not purchased new, what warranty work was required to bring the machine up to standard, and was it then satisfactory?

Super Profile

DF. The original dealer would not carry out the 500 mile service because of the machine's age, without making a charge. So I carried out the service myself and have since done all my own work as the machine is easy to work on. Luckily there were no problems that would have necessitated a warranty claim.
JRN. Have you experienced difficulty in obtaining parts? What solutions, if any, did you find necessary?
DF. I have not had any problems with parts. There are many Triumph dealers in North West London.
JRN. What kind of handling and performance does your machine provide?
DF. I like the handling. The only problem is in grounding the centre stand when cornering, which could account for the breakages. Low speed torque provides good acceleration; I embarrassed a friend on a 750 Honda by out-accelerating him in top gear!
JRN. Is the bike in continual use? How practical is it – are the running costs high?
DF. I use it every day for work. It is reasonably economical, slim and easy to handle in traffic Some spares are expensive. I expect about 40mpg in town, and 65mpg on a run. The machine has always burnt oil, which averages about 400 miles per pint. I did once use a pint in 100 miles to Dover, when in a hurry!
JRN. How helpful is it to be a member of the Triumph Owners MCC?
DF. There is a useful discount when parts are purchased. I regret I am not an active member.
JRN. Is there a specialist you have found particularly helpful?
DF. Roebuck Motors, of Rayners Lane, is my local dealer. He has 99% of the parts for my model in stock.
JRN. How much enjoyment do you get from your machine?
DF. This depends on how much trouble it is causing at the time!
JRN. What advice would you give to potential Bonneville Owners?
DF. Ignore comments from your Jap bike-riding friends!

My final interview was with Fred Quinton, of Romsey, Hampshire, who is 'on the wrong side' of fifty and has returned to motorcycling after forsaking it in 1957 when he got married, had to raise a mortgage, started a family and bought a car. When his daughter acquired a bike, he started to get interested again, and after a brief encounter with a Japanese 250, he decided to buy British and acquired a new Triumph in 1980. His comments are of particular interest, as he first started riding in 1947, when 99% of the bikes on the road were of British manufacture.

JRN. Why are you so interested in the Bonneville?
FQ. When I resumed motorcycling, I bought a Japanese 250, but I soon got fed up with it and decided I had to have a British bike as I could not be proud of a machine with a Japanese name on the tank.
JRN. When and why did you buy your Bonnie?
FQ. I bought it new in April 1980, as Triumph were the only firm still making a British motorcycle.
JRN. What condition was it in? If you found faults, were these common problems?
FQ. As I bought new, this question does not really apply.
JRN. What repairs/renovation work has been done, and what advice would you give to someone facing similar problems?
FQ. I found the electrical switches left a lot to be desired, so I scrapped the indicator, horn and headlamp flash switches, using a Ford electric aerial switch for the indicators, which centralises when released. In place of the horn and starter switches I fitted a micro switch, with two relays in the headlamp. As a result, I now have reliable indicators, horn and headlamp flash switches. The silencers quickly rusted through at the reverse cone ends, so I cut these off and the silencers are still going strong. The paint on the frame peeled off, so I touched this in. The petrol tank paintwork was poor, but I have since had this repainted to my own design. Oil leaks are difficult to cure for any length of time and the clutch drags, which spoils an otherwise nice gearbox.
JRN. If purchased new, what warranty work was required to bring the machine up to standard, and was it then satisfactory?
FQ. Warranty work was minimal, namely fixing an oil leak from the front forks and a faulty ignition switch. After the 500 mile service, the primary chain was too slack and it took up all the adjustment to get it correct.
JRN. Have you experienced difficulty in obtaining parts? What solutions, if any, did you find necessary?
FQ. I have found Globe Motorcycles, of Fawcett Road, Southsea, to be very helpful. They know British bikes and take an interest in seeing that you get the correct part.
JRN. What kind of handling and performance does your machine provide?
FQ. I have no criticisms of the handling of my Bonnie at all. It handles well on cornering, staying on the same course even when it is laid right over. It is also predictable over pot-holes and manhole covers. Performance, though not comparable with a Japanese machine of the same engine capacity, is adequate for today's conditions and speed limitations. The Triumph scores highly on petrol consumption; on a long run I have had over 70mpg cruising at about 70mph, two-up, although the normal average is about 55-65mpg.
JRN. Is the bike in continual use? How practical is it – are the running costs high?
FQ. My bike is not used during the winter months (usually a three month period). During the summer, I suppose I average about 300/400

Super Profile

miles per week, comprising about 200 miles for business purposes and the rest on Sundays, for pleasure. My wife is as keen as I am. Last year we took the Triumph to Italy on holiday, and hope to go to Austria on it in September this year. With regard to running costs, some replacement parts such as tyres, brake pads and batteries are more expensive than their counterparts for cars, yet need to be replaced just as frequently. Chains do not last long either, even when they are well looked-after. My actual expenditure, from April to March each year was: 1980/1, £30 for 9,000 miles, 1981/2, £131 for 12,000 miles, 1982/3, £226 for 9,000 miles, 1983/4, £228 for 16,000 miles. My overall gain has been on petrol consumption. Had I have covered these annual mileages in a car, the overall cost would have been about £2-3,000 more, a lot more than I paid for the bike.

JRN. How helpful is it to be a member of the Triumph Owners MCC?

FQ. I doubt whether membership has proved particularly helpful, apart from the fact that we all share a common interest. Membership would probably be of more use if one had an older bike, with regard to where to obtain parts to help with restoration.

JRN. Is there a specialist you have found to be particularly helpful?

FQ. Globe Motorcycles, as mentioned above.

JRN. How much enjoyment do you get from your machine?

FQ. Both my wife and I get a great deal of pleasure out of the bike. I suppose at our ages we should know better, but we do genuinely get a great deal of fun and enjoyment out of riding it.

JRN. What advice would you give to potential Bonneville owners?

FQ. To be a potential Bonnie owner I would say you need to keep the machine well maintained and to keep a weather eye open for potential troubles. If you can nip problems in the bud, you will have a machine that is a joy to ride, and one that is long lived. Also, it is not affected by changes in fashion. You will belong to a group of people who are British bike enthusiasts, and they are a pretty friendly bunch.

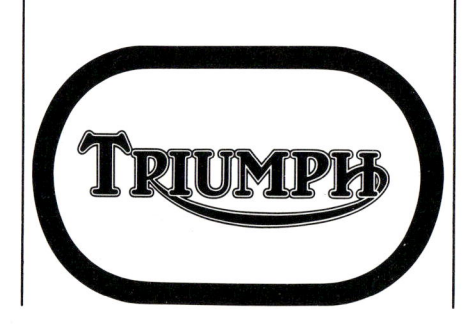

Super Profile

BUYING

The lifetime of the Bonneville covers a quarter of a century and naturally, the older the particular model is, the rarer, and thus the more sought after it becomes. One sad fact is that the very early Bonnevilles suffered the 1960s craze of 'chopping', often resulting in frame and fork conversions together with strange engine modifications that preclude a return to original condition, no matter what the effort.

Most riders enjoy adapting their machine to suit their own style, but beware the offer of a "genuine original specification" model without having swotted up the details previously! The writer has often received photographs of machines lovingly restored to an unrecognisable non-genuine specification.

However, there are very few problems in obtaining 'wearing' parts, as there is an almost worldwide industry in pattern and Far East equivalents, and the vendor doesn't always warn of the pitfalls of non-genuine replacements.

The other great advantage of choosing a Triumph is that most of the components that normally suffer were made of materials that can be straightened, bored, welded, polished, sleeved, chromed, heli-coiled, and the crankcases and gearboxes accept off-the-shelf bearings, pistons, rings, valves, guides, springs etc, so that the basic skeleton — although perhaps a trifle primitive by today's standards of technology — is still readily reconditionable at very economical cost.

A Triumph engine, when carefully assembled, remains oil tight. It is perhaps one of its failings that its simplicity of construction has for years tempted the uninitiated to have-a-go and subsequently drown their inefficiency in oil! Today, with modern jointing compounds and sealants, even the most maltreated early joint faces should provide a reliable long term seal. A Triumph is every bit as good as the guy who puts it together!

Some years models suffered their own in-built unreliabilities. Early twin contact breaker machines, following the demise of the magneto, experienced piston holing and pre-ignition problems. Electrics were perennially unreliable with ammeters going open circuit or distintegrating. Even that great leap forward, the introduction of electronic ignition, was marred by failures caused by unwarranted unreliability of small integral but seemingly insignificant components (like unprotected bullet connectors).

On the other side of the coin, two notable successes have withstood the test of time — encapsulation of the alternator stator (rotors *always* remained burstable) and the introduction of nitrided camshafts — not one of which, it can be said, in the hundreds of thousands to have been made since, has been known to wear out, hitherto almost a regular feature.

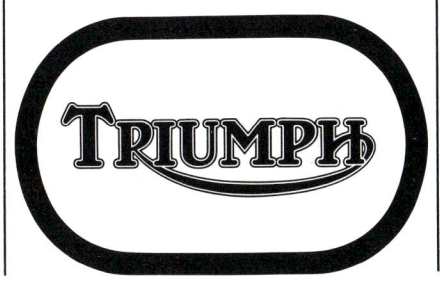

The introduction of Zener Diode-controlled electrical systems in 1966 eliminated once and for all the switched output to suit pre-determined electrical load conditions (hopefully) and is recommended to be adopted on any 1963/6 models under review for reconditioning or restoration.

The Bonneville has always been a thoroughbred, and as such, responds in accordance with the care and attention given to it. A well cared for Bonneville is at least every bit as good, if not better, than most of equivalent stature, capacity or price, and will repay a careful owner with many years of secure and reliable service. There were a lot of them around, so the choice remains reasonably wide, but because the Bonnie was always popular, not only are the motorcycles generally readily available — often in excellent condition, and therefore reasonably cheap to buy, but because of the spares potential involved, there remains a reasonable world-wide supply of economical replacement spare parts.

Taking the four distinct periods of the 650 cc Bonneville, and the two eras of the 750 cc, a brief summary of the particular features to look for is as follows:

1959 One year's production only with Tangerine and Pearl Grey in the first half, and Royal Blue and Pearl Grey the second half. The separate engined pre-unit construction model had magneto ignition and a dynamo, but the nacelle was considered too fussy for a sports machine. Flywheel bolt breakage not unknown.

1960/1/2 Continuing with pre-unit construction engine and gearbox, but now with lightweight duplex cradle frame. The magneto continued, but switched alternator lighting brought its own complication and service problems.

29

Super Profile

1963-70 Unit construction engine and gearbox with new single downtube frame. Fitted from the beginning with duplex primary chain, nine stud cylinder head and barrel, hinged twinseat and the ill-fated twin contact breaker and "emergency" starting specification, but reliability enhanced year by year. 12 volt electrics and enscapulated stator in 1966, nitrided camshafts in 1969. The 1969 series has since been generally accepted as the best year of the 650 cc models.

1971-74 The Umberslade retrogressive step backwards, gradually improving in specification and reliability up to 1974. Specified triplex primary chain, 5 speed gearbox option. The 'oil-in-frame' frame was at first weak and unreliable, but a series of subsequent modifications over two years produced a set standard that endured to the last of the breed. The front drum brake was hopeless until the arrival of the disc in 1973. The rear drum brake remained unusable. 650s and 750s co-existed in 71 to 74.

1975-83 The reliability and specification improved as the Co-operative climbed the learning curve! Left foot shift and rear disc brake. The 650cc died its natural, when Jubilees and Electric Starts were born. The Electric Start endured three variants before overcoming its teething troubles (sic) and sadly the A.V. model never reached real production. Those who now own a TSS AV conversion say that without doubt, this was the finest of them all!!

Super Profile

CLUBS, SPECIALISTS & BOOKS

Clubs

The Triumph Owners Motorcycle Club has, since its formation in 1949, been actively engaged in furthering the collective interest of Triumph owning motorcyclists and the organisation of voluntary local events and happenings from Branch level, to those of international status.

Membership is open to all owners of any Triumph-engined motorcycle, and although the Bonneville itself does not lay claim to a specific club or branch of its own, as does say, the three cylinder Triumph Trident, the Bonnie does seem to predominate as the 'members' choice'.

The Club exists to enable its members to get together at weekly or monthly meetings, with shows, displays, talks, discussions or simply, just a pleasant evening spent talking motorcycles or about future club activities. Each Branch elects its own committee together with officials such as Events Organiser and Branch Secretary.

The intensity of interest and activity depends on the collective enthusiasm and endeavours of the individual members in each branch, but normally in addition to the indoor social activities, most branches venture into organising charity work, local club runs, participation in rallies, displays, shows and concours events, and many provide emergency services.

All members are kept well abreast of forthcoming events through the excellent and comprehensive thirty-paged monthly club magazine, named in commemoration of that always admired Triumph feature *The Nacelle*. Each issue contains local branch activity reports, dates, times and venues of local and national meetings, features and sections covering Triumph hints and tips, members' letters and literary contributions, for sale and wanted ads and of course the inevitable but essentially useful Triumph specialist workshop advertisements.

There are overseas branches or representatives in the USA, Australia, New Zealand and Spain. If, however, the enthusiastic owner is an itinerant of no fixed abode, and would still appreciate the satisfaction of becoming a Club member, then the Headquarters Branch will keep him fully informed and within their sights as he journeys the world.

The Club elects its own officers, including President, Vice-Presidents, Chairman and Treasurer, with its own Secretary and Assistant Secretary, co-ordinating the combined administration of the thirty nine Branches, with the additional positions of Magazine Editor, Social Secretary, Competitions Secretary, P.R.O., ACU and BMF Representatives, an essential and integral part of the very well run yet professionally co-ordinated voluntary activities.

The Club also boasts a comprehensive library of Triumph technical literature and information, under the care and custody of the Club's own elected Librarian, the existence of such a position being indicative of members' depth of interest, but being essential not only to guide enquiring members with genuine authoritative technical help with their own query or problem, but to settle the inevitable technical challenges that somehow always seem to be generated when motorcyclists are rubbed together to discuss their favourite subject.

The Triumph Owners Motorcycle Club
Club Secretary: Roy Shilling, 66 Oaklands Avenue, Heanor, Derby DE7 7BB. Tel: 0773 763940
Assistant Secretary: Mrs Edna Page, 101 Great Knightleys, Basildon, Essex SS15 5AN Tel: 0268 285100
H.Q. Branch Secretary: Mrs Maureen Baxter, 54 South Drive, Brentwood, Essex. Tel: 0277 210937
U.K. Branches: Aylesbury – Bedford – Berkshire – Bexley – Birmingham and Wolverhampton – Bristol – Chorley – Cotswold – Epping Forest – Furness – Great Yarmouth – **Headquarters** – Ilford – Ipswich – Jersey C.I. – Leicester – Liverpool – Manchester – Medway – Meriden – Mid. Surrey – Northampton – North West London – Nottingham – Plymouth – Rother – Scottish – South Dorset – South Hants – South London – South Wales – Tyre & Wear – Weald – Wessex – West Middlesex – West Riding – West Sussex – Wirral – Yorkshire Rose.
Overseas Branches: Australia
Overseas Representatives: New Zealand, Spain, USA

31

Super Profile

Specialists

Despite the supply problems over the past years, there are still motorcycle dealers who specialise in British-built motorcycles, and even restrict their loyalty to the one Triumph brand.

Below is a list of a number of those who have earned the reputation of being able to find those elusive parts that other dealers cannot be bothered to reach.

Anglo-Bike,
Beenham Garage,
Beenham,
Nr Reading,
Berkshire.
Tel: 0734 382

Reg Allan,
39/41 Grosvenor Road,
Hanwell,
London, W7.
Tel: 01-567 1974

Brit-Bits (Ray Fisher Motorcycles) Ltd.,
185 Barrack Road
Christchurch,
Dorset,
Tel: 0202 483675

Charlie's (R.A. Hall),
169-171 Fishponds Road,
Eastville,
Bristol, BS5 2PR.
Tel: 0272 511019

Richard Hacker Motorcycles,
18-19 Green Lane,
Penge,
London, SE20
Tel: 01 659 4045

Hamrax Motors Ltd,
328 Ladbroke Grove,
North Kensington,
London, W10.
Tel: 01 969 5380

High Gear Motorcycles,
217 Streatham Road,
Mitcham,
Surrey, CR4 2AJ
Tel: 01 648 2900

Jacksons Garage,
Edward Street,
Chorley,
Lancs, PR6 0RC
Tel: 02572 64151

Kays of Ealing,
10 Bond Street,
London, W5
Tel: 01 567 2387

Revetts (Norwich Rd) Ltd,
53-67 Norwich Road,
Ipswich 1Pl 2ER
Tel: 0473 53726

Roebuck Motorcycles,
354 Rayners Lane,
Pinner,
Middlesex, HA5 5EP
Tel: 01 868 1232

Carl Rosner,
Station Approach,
Sanderstead,
South Croydon,
Surrey
Tel: 01 657 0121

T.M.S. of Nottingham,
92/94 Carlton Road,
Nottingham, NG2 2AS
Tel: 0602 503447

Wilmans Motors,
Siddals Road,
Derby, DE1 2P2
Tel: 0332 42813

Restoration
Hughie Hancox Restorations,
(The Triumph Specialist),
11 Burbury Close,
Marston Lane,
Bedworth,
Warwickshire, CV12 8DU
Tel: 0203 310211

J.W. Tennant Eyles,
Barcote Manor,
Buckland,
Nr Faringdon,
Oxfordshire, SN7 8PP
Tel: 036787 330

High Performance Kits
Norman Hyde,
Rigby Close,
Heathcote,
Warwick, CV34 GTL
Tel: 0926 497375

Books

'Bonnie' – The Development History of the Triumph Bonneville by J.R. Nelson. Published by the Haynes Publishing Group, Sparkford, Nr. Yeovil, Somerset, BA22 7JJ, England.

It's a Triumph by Ivor Davies. A history of the Triumph company, featuring over 300 photographs. Published by the Haynes Group, Sparkford, Nr. Yeovil, Somerset, BA22 7JJ, England.

Triumph Twins and Triples by Roy Bacon. An accurate and informative addition to the Osprey Collector's Library series. Published by Osprey Publishing Ltd, 12-14, Long Acre, London, WC2E 9LP, England.

The Story of Triumph Motorcycles by Bob Currie and Harry Louis. Published by Patrick Stephens Ltd, Barr Hill, Cambridge, England.

The above titles can be obtained from several booksellers who specialise in motorcycle titles, including:-

Bruce Main-Smith Retail Ltd,
P.O. Box 20,
Leatherhead,
Surrey,
England.
Tel: 0372 375615

Mill House Books,
Mill House,
Eastville,
Boston,
Lincs, PE22 8LS,
England.
Tel: 020 584 377

Super Profile

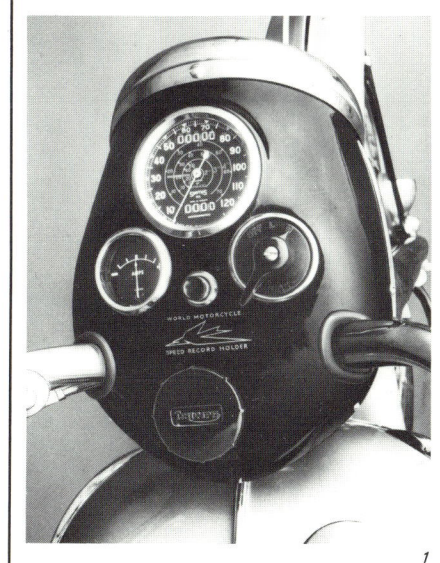

PHOTO GALLERY

1. The World Motorcycle Speed Record 'Thunderbird' motif that was applied to all Triumph models subsequent to Johnny Allen's successful record breaking attempt in 1956.

2. Johnny Allen preparing to board the streamliner in which he broke the World's Speed Record at Bonneville Salt Flats on 6th September 1956. This photograph was taken at Wellesbourne aerodrome in Warwickshire immediately prior to the streamliner's debut at the Earls Court Motor Cycle Show in November 1956. It is now on permanent display at the National Motorcycle Museum at Bickenhill, in Warwickshire.

3. The original FIM Certificate confirming Johnny Allen's success in achieving the World's Motorcycle Speed Record – the basis of the Triumph claim as a World's Speed Record holder. It was the event that gave the Triumph Bonneville its name. This was the only FIM-confirmed record; all those that were to follow were AMA records.

FEDERATION INTERNATIONALE MOTOCYCLISTE

TELEPHONE: HAWKHURST 2178
TELEGRAMS:
LOUGHBOROUGH, HAWKHURST, ENGLAND

SECRETARY GENERAL:
T. W. LOUGHBOROUGH, A.M.I.Mech.E.

THE OLD FORGE,
HAWKHURST,
KENT, ENGLAND
17th September, 1956.

RECORD NOTICE No. 56/13

The Federation has this day been advised of the following results of recent attempts at World's Record. These claims to World's Records are found to be in order, and, subject to no protest being received within three months from date will automatically and finally be confirmed as :-

WORLD'S RECORDS

DATE :- 6th September, 1956   PLACE :- Bonneville Salt Flats, UTAH, U.S.A.
DRIVER :- Mr. John ALLEN
MOTORCYCLE :- TRIUMPH 'Streamliner' Motorbicycle, with a two-cylinder four-stroke engine, not supercharged, bore 71.04 x stroke 81.94 mm. = 649.56 c.c.
Classification :- Category A, Class 750.

RESULTS :-

	Sec.	Km.p.h.	M.p.h.	Existing Record (Herz, 2.8.1956) Sec.	Km.p.h.	M.p.h.
(1) f.s. 1 Km.	10.4	345	214	10.6	338	210
(4) f.s. 1 Mile	16.8	345	214½	17.1	339	211

Each of the above records also gained record in Class A.1000.
The results for the flying mile are the fastest ever officially recorded for any class or distance.

SECRETARY GENERAL.

33

Super Profile

4. The clean lines presented by the nacelle, handlebar and controls are well illustrated in this view of the 'first of the Bonnevilles'. Seen also are the tank top parcel grid, deep valanced front mudguard, and the traditional Triumph 'picture framed' front number plate incorporating the chromed outer bezelled rim.

5. The first season's T120 model 650cc Bonnevilles fitted this narrow 'sports' dualseat in conjunction with downswept handlebars. As the machine was being offered to riders of great experience, capable of handling its potential (said the adverts), it was quite a departure in those days of strict Triumph touring ideology to offer these concessions to such a racey image.

Super Profile

6. How's that for restoration? Restored for eventual display in the National Motorcycle Museum at Bickenhill, this 1959 Bonneville has been rebuilt with obvious loving care and faithful attention to detail by Hughie Hancox, formerly a member of the Triumph Service Department's repair shop staff.

7. The pleasing, burbling note emitted by the $1\frac{3}{4}$ inch diameter exhaust pipes and small silencers is no longer evident in the silencing arrangements of today's machines. Except, of course, for those capable of restoring a machine to the beautiful condition of the one shown here.

8. The first 1959 Bonnevilles were considered almost outrageous in their day, providing an unnecessary sporting image. Nevertheless, even today, the basically classic lines have lost little with the passing of time and fashion.

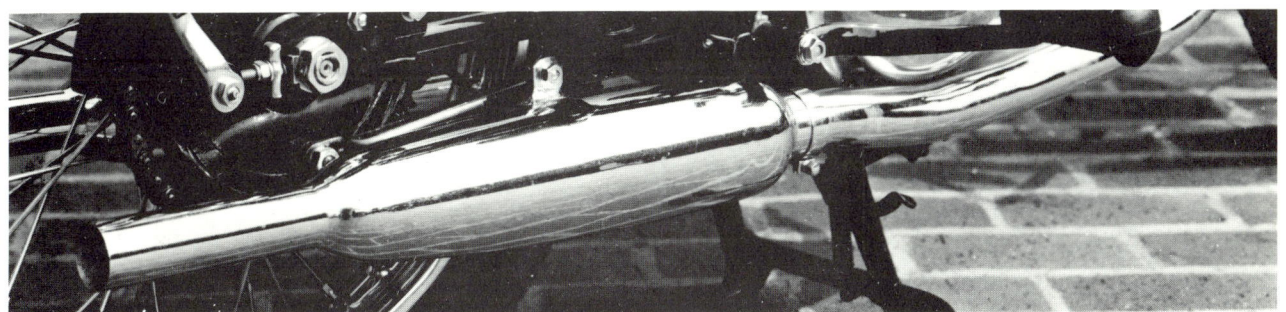

Super Profile

9. The engine-driven Lucas dynamo disappeared in favour of an AC generator after the first 1959 season model, as shown here. But the Lucas K2F magneto was retained until the introduction of coil ignition and twin contact breakers in 1963.

10. The 1959 Bonneville T120, the only year to have a nacelle and deep valanced mudguards. Although 'pre-unit construction' in 1959, the separate engine and gearbox were built into a single front down tube frame. This was revised to a duplex tube frame until the 'unit-construction' engines appeared, which were then fitted into a brand new single down tube frame once again.

11. The clean lines of the 1959 front wheel 8 inch diameter full-width single leading shoe brake drum, fitted into front forks devoid of unsightly lugs and bracketry. This type of hub continued to be fitted until the 1966 season.

12. The Amal 'chopped off' Monobloc Amal carburettor on pre-unit construction models really did have the essentially 'monobloc' float bowl portion cleanly removed and replaced by a flexibly-mounted remote central float bowl to counter any engine vibration, and thereby reduce aeration, aid fuel flow and maintain the correct level under extreme conditions.

13. Three-quarters rear view of the right-hand side of the 1959 Bonneville, which gives a good impression of the depth of valance incorporated into the rear mudguard, affording anti-splash protection never to be repeated on later models. Also the Q.D. wheel as shown was quickly detachable – the wheel spindle could be withdrawn without recourse to silencer removal, not unknown on later models. (But the bike required tilting to thread the wheel clear of the silencer).

Super Profile

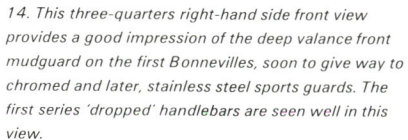

14. This three-quarters right-hand side front view provides a good impression of the deep valance front mudguard on the first Bonnevilles, soon to give way to chromed and later, stainless steel sports guards. The first series 'dropped' handlebars are seen well in this view.

15. Known as the 'mouth organ' petrol tank badge, it blended well with the overall design presentation. The nacelle housing the control cables, electrical wiring and handlebar mounts, and providing a clean and streamlined instrument panel, was not quite so appreciated by the technician seeking a mysterious intermittent electrical fault.

16. The 1960 model Bonneville as chosen for the US market. The nacelle has now given way to a chromed, domed headlamp shell mounted on integral fork headlamp brackets. The dynamo has been superseded by an ac alternator within the primary chaincase and for intended competition use, a crankcase undershield, sports mudguards and twin upswept exhaust pipes and silencers have been fitted. The success of this model in the hands of American tuners and riders led to the overwhelming success of the later TT model series.

17. The first Bonnevilles built by the factory for the Thruxton 500 mile production race were a quantity of ten that came off the main assembly line in late April 1959. Pre-unit engines in the duplex frame were made in 1960, 1961 and 1962. The model featured in the photograph is a 1961 Bonneville converted to Thruxton specification, using the currently available kit parts. The rider astride the bike is John Holder, and shaking a congratulatory hand from Ivor Davies, Triumph's Publicity Manager, is Tony Godfrey, his partner in a consistently successful racing pairing.

Super Profile

18. Marshalling the marshals. It became almost custom and practice in the mid-50s and early 60s for Triumph to supply the machines for the Isle of Man TT Travelling Marshals.

19. Bonneville, Utah – 25th August 1961. Gary Richards, a 20 year old Triumph rider who, on a 650cc Bonneville T120 model achieved a new Class AA record (production motorcycle burning alcohol fuel) of 159.542mph, beating his previous record of 149.513mph. During this final attempt, Gary ran at 160.272mph in one direction. What he did not know on that day was that his record was to remain unbroken for the next five years.

20. Cameras roll! Action! 'Young' Bill Johnson in the Joe Dudek streamliner taken at the start of the World's Record attempt in August 1962. By the end of the day Bill had successfully claimed the World's Motorcycle Speed Record at 230.269mph.

21. The Johnson-Dudek record holder. Left to right: Wilbur Ceder, President of Johnson Motors Inc, Bill Johnson, rider, Joe Dudek, builder of the Triumph streamliner shell, and Earl Flanders, supervisor of the World's Record established under the auspices of the American Motorcycle Association at 230.269mph, the two-way average over a measured mile course. At that time Triumph also held additional unbroken 650cc US National Records achieved at Bonneville, whilst five other National speed records dating back from 1958 in the 200cc, 350cc and 500cc categories were certified valid at this time.

Super Profile

22. An informal shot of 'young' Bill Johnson, so called because the President of Johnson Motors Inc. who sponsored the World's Record attempt, also has the same name.

23. The Triumph Corporation in America, based at Baltimore in Maryland, ran regular dealer mechanic schools to train and upgrade the support for the product in the field. These were always well represented, and here Cliff Guild is seen conducting a class in the Baltimore schoolroom. The subject under review, and their immediate interest is, of course, the Bonneville.

24. Triumph and BSA headquarters for the west coast of America, situated at Duarte, Los Angeles, California.

25. A Thruxton Bonneville with 'chopped off' Amal Monobloc carburettors and remote carburettor float bowl. Always a very limited production model, the Thruxton Bonneville incorporated the competitive 'goodies' which, by 1966, 7 and 8 had expanded to full factory racing equipment. This included alloy wheel rims, fuel and oil tanks etc., after which (and inevitably) the Production Class became a race of the 'giants', leaving little chance for the amateur or individual production race privateer.

26. Bonnevilles for the Sydney police. The first truckload of T120 Bonneville police machines leaves the Triumph factory at Meriden in 1963, escorted by a team of Triumph testers riding later machines from the same consignment, prior to final adjustments, packing and despatch to Australia.

39

Super Profile

27

28

29

30

27. The 1963 version of the T120 Bonneville model, now in unit-construction form, with a brand new robust single front down tube frame. With only minor seasonal changes, it continued until the end of the 1970 season. This particular model was finished with an Alaskan White tank and guards, and all other parts painted in Black.

28. The Bonneville TT Special, fitted with 11:1 compression ratio pistons and $1\frac{3}{8}$ inch choke Amal carburettors, with $1\frac{3}{4}$ inch diameter straight-through exhaust pipes. The 1965 US catalogue quoted the American Motorcycle Association's confirmation that this limited production model was the winner of more 'TT' races than all other makes combined.

29. Eddie Mulder in the lead again! Aboard his 1963 650cc unit-construction T120 model Bonneville at the Ascot Raceway in the 1963 TT event. It was the success at this National and in similar events on the west coast of America that resulted in factory production during 1964 of the 'out-of-the-crate' US TT Special model. In 1966 Eddie won three National Championship races, all on the same T120 TT model.

30. Eddie was also the American West Coast Scrambles Champion. Here he is seen ahead of the opposition in a 1965 desert enduro event.

Super Profile

31. Steve McQueen, Triumph enthusiast, Bonneville owner, star of screen and television, motorcycling sportsman and International Six Days Trial participant in the first American Team – on a Triumph of course! Here he is seen on his own Bonneville.

32. L to R: Kenneth H. Dopps, of Ken's Motor Sport, Bellevue, Washington, Theodore J. Dupee of Cycle City in Gorst, Washington, John Nelson, World Service Manager for Triumph Engineering Company Ltd, of Coventry, England, and Cal Brown, Service Manager for Johnson Motors Inc., Pasadena, California, inspect the new 1966 Bonneville T120 model at the 28th Annual Western Dealers Meeting held in the Huntington-Sheraton Hotel in Pasadena on 20th September 1965.

33. A romantic picture taken in a romantic setting. The original of this photograph taken at Arbury Hall in Warwickshire featured in the 1965 US catalogue. By now the Triumph slogan had been amended to 'The World's Best and Fastest Motorcycle'!

Super Profile

34. The 1966 Bonneville T120R in Alaskan White, with Bronze-lined Grenadier Red petrol tank central 'racing stripe'. Stainless steel mudguards were introduced for the first time on US models.

35. Bob Leppan with Gyronaut X-1, the last of a long line of Triumph-powered 'fastest'. In August 1966 Bob achieved the AMA-approved record on two-wheels of 245.667mph. He continued to hold this until his final attempt on 20th October 1970, when he achieved 264.437mph – sanctioned by the American Motorcycle Association and timed by the United States Auto Club.

36. Choose your own Bonneville! Triumph testers about to start a day's work. Envied by all in summer, but by none in the depths of winter. The writer does recall severe winter weather conditions when even these stalwarts chose not to operate. On one such occasion, to their shame, they witnessed the arrival through the deeply-packed snow of a diminutive slip of a girl on her own Bonnie!

Super Profile

37. Skip Van Leeuwin in action. Skip was one of the formidable contenders for the crown in US west coast flat track and 'TT' events. He is seen here in typical action on his Bonneville TT Special in the 30 lap National Championship Race at Ascot Park, Gardena, California in July 1966, where he finished third.

38. Just a good photograph that has to be included. An informal short of Triumph's Percy Tait caught enjoying a smile with Giacomo Agostini. The moment is enhanced by the background photograph portraying the great John Hartle on No.7, winning the first ever Production TT on a Bonneville in 1967.

39. No story of the Bonneville in the USA could be completed without a fine action picture of Gary Nixon. He earned, and retained, the US number one racing plate over many years, winning on Triumph Cubs, Tigers and Bonnies, including the famous Daytona win in 1967. He is seen here on the west coast on his TT model in the 50 lap TT National Championship at Ascot in 1968. On this occasion he finished 8th.

40. Sir Geoffrey Tuttle, President of the British Motor Cycle Racing Club, presents the Mellano Trophy, the premier classic award of the British racing year, to John Hartle, who on 13th August 1967 won the Hutchinson 100 race on a standard production Bonneville at 83.37mph. John had the double distinction that year of also being the winner of the 1967 Isle of Man Production TT Race on a Triumph Bonneville, a magnificent achievement for both man and machine.

41. An interesting photograph of part of the rig used by Evel Knievel when incorporating his jet thrusters to jump the Grand Canyon. Note the ejector seat and parachute.

Super Profile

42. Find the Bonneville! Evel Knievel in full flight jumping 16 cars during the 20 Mile National Championships at Portland, Oregon, on 16th July, 1967.

43. Have you ever wondered what happens to the multiplicity of publicity shots that never again appear – and why? Here's one that didn't, taken on the Triumph stand at the Belle Vue Motor Cycle Show at Manchester in 1968. Standing firm on the deck, stiffly to attention, thumbs in line and under very close review by a crew of shapely twins, is Peter Britton, the Triumph Export Manager. The subject of their pride is the 1968 home specification Bonneville twin bearing on the tool box cover the coveted emblem of the 1967 Queen's Award to Industry for Export Achievement.

44. A happy World Champion, Mike Hailwood, aboard the motorcycle of his own choice, a 1968 Bonneville T120R model. The finish is Hi-Fi Scarlet petrol tank, with chromed steel mudguards.

45. The camera clicks, and even a British Ambassador can be caught letting his hair down! His Excellency Sir John Russell is seen supporting the British export drive in Sao Paulo, Brazil, in 1968, aboard a Bonneville at the British Industrial Exhibition.

46. 1968 models had a simple 3-way lighting toggle switch fitted in the headlamp, working in conjunction with the ignition switch seen mounted on the left-hand fork headlamp mounting bracket. The Metalastic-mounted Smiths matching speedometer and tachometer had always featured on this model. The warning lights indicate ignition/oil pressure and the main beam.

47. The 1968 twin leading shoe front brake with cooling airscoop. Problems were experienced in service with the operating cable and abutment retention. The mechanism was amended for 1969.

Super Profile

48. Percy Tait trying hard as usual in the 500 Miles Grand Prix d'Endurance Race held during 1968.

49. Malcolm Uphill on his way to victory in the 750cc class on his 650cc T120 factory-entered Bonneville in the 1969 Isle of Man Production Machine TT Race. He was awarded the John Hartle Challenge Trophy for a record lap speed on his second lap at 100.37mph, and his overall winning race speed at the record of 99.99mph. This was the first production motorcycle ever to lap the Isle of Man TT course at over 100mph.

50. Third place in the historic 1969 TT Production Machine Race was taken by Dale Pendlebury on his T120 Bonneville, entered by Alec Bennett of Southampton. The Doug Hele plan was bearing fruit, and the 1966 and 1967 successes with the winning Daytona Tiger 100s were continuing with the 650cc Bonneville models.

51. I'll take that one! Freddie Frith approves of Dick Emery's choice of a Bonneville in 1969. Photograph taken by the Grimsby Evening Telegraph to commemorate Emery's visit to this famous Triumph dealer in Grimsby on 29th May that year.

52. The 1969 twin leading shoe front brake with redesigned brake lever actuating mechanism. The new levers maintained the operating cable in line with the fork sliding member.

53. The 1969 Bonneville rear end. This was the first year the name on the tool box lid was spelled out in block capitals, and not in copperplate, as the previous 'Bonneville 120' motif.

54. The 1969 Bonneville, now fitted with twin windtone horns for the first time, also fitted Orange side reflectors for the USA, to meet Federal legislative requirements.

55. The coupled exhaust pipe system was introduced on 1969 Bonnevilles, effectively assisting exhaust gas flow and reducing noise emissions. The high-tensile 12-point cylinder base holding nuts had been introduced the previous year, finally providing adequate spanner clearance!

Super Profile

56. Another famous name with which to conjure. Ray Pickrell aboard his 650cc Triumph Bonneville in Thruxton trim in the 1970 Brands Hatch 500 Mile event. Although the Bonnie continued its competitive success, the advent of the 750cc three cylinder Trident T150 model in 1969 provided further opportunity for Doug Hele and his racing team to maintain the success of Triumph in the field of competition. By now, the 650cc Bonneville was reaching its peak of competitive potential.

57. The last of the Triumph Engineering Company's own design, a 1970 model in Astral Red and Silver 'swept wing' central tank panel motif. The mudguards were also finished in Astral Red.

58. Change of corporate image was brought about by amending the Triumph logo introduced by the BSA Group in 1970.

59. Triumph's own race ace, Percy Tait. For many years the chief experimental and development tester at Meriden, he won a world reputation for consistent leader board results. Here he is seen trickling a 1971 Bonneville over the sand on a beach in Wales.

60. The illustration shows the 1971 T120 Bonneville, known subsequently as the 'Umberslade' model, due to its unacceptably high frame and other retrograde features. By 1973 the frame had changed to one of manageable proportions, and a front disc brake incorporated into the specification which, together with more conventional side panels and fork headlamp mountings again attempted to satisfy the traditional Bonneville owner.

TRIUMPH BONNEVILLE 650

Super Profile

61. The first of the 'Umberslade' Bonnevilles. The 1971 US version of the T120 model is shown here, with the duplex front down tube 'oil in frame' facility which continued to be made at Meriden until the cessation of production in 1983.

62. The 1971 silencer and alloy rear wheel hub and drum brake.

63. The 1971 'Umberslade' eight inch twin leading shoe front hub and drum brake. It was rapidly superseded by a front disc brake to restore braking efficiency.

64. The 1976/77 Bonneville, the first to be produced by the Meriden Co-operative, and the first with left-hand footchange and rear disc brake. It was available from that time onward only as a 750cc model equipped with a 5-speed gearbox. The above model is to US specification.

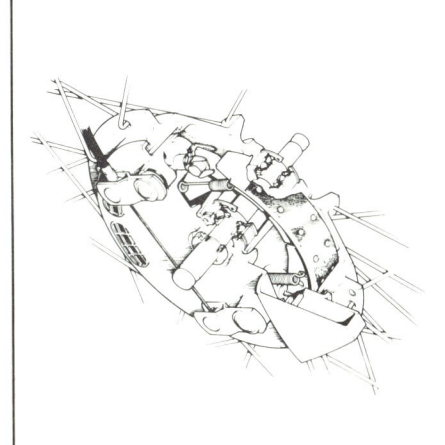

Super Profile

65

65. The US export version of the 1977 Silver Jubilee T140V model. The motif on the side cover proclaims 'one of a thousand'. In fact, a quantity of one thousand home specification models were manufactured, a further one thousand for the US market, and a further small quantity for the ex-colonies. 'She's our Queen as well, you know', insisted the ex-colonials!

66. The 1980 T140E Bonneville American is identified by the tank finish, Scarlet with Black panels lined in Gold, as shown here, and the repositioning of the rear brake caliper above the wheel centre line. The significance of the letter 'E' in the model designation confirms its compliance with the strict US exhaust emission legislative requirements.

67. The last of the Bonnevilles to be made at Meriden. The 1983 TSS 750cc model with the Weslake 8-valve cylinder head shown here in the 'AV' frame is fitted with twin front brake discs and cast aluminium wheels. The engine had a 9:1 compression ratio, and was fitted with twin Amal Mark II Concentric carburettors, electronic ignition and electric start. A 5-speed gearbox was fitted as standard, the wheel and tyre diameters being 4.10 x 18 inch front and 4.25 x 18 inch rear, in conjunction with Strada rear shock absorber units.

68. The company slogan between the two world wars was simply 'The World's Pre-eminent Motorcycle'. This was superseded in 1946 with the above unequivocal claim that appeared on all sales and publicity literature up to the closure of the Triumph Engineering Company Limited in 1973.

66

67

68

The Best Motorcycle in the World

48

Super Profile

C1

C2

C1. The 1959 model Bonneville, finished in two-tone Tangerine and Pearl Grey, has been beautifully restored to its original condition and is to be seen on permanent display at the National Motorcycle Museum at Bickenhill, in Warwickshire. It is the proud possession of the Museum founder, Roy Richards, of Catherine de Barnes, near Solihull.

C2. The left-hand side view of the same machine, illustrating the great care and accuracy employed in the task of renovation. Later models in the 1959 series were finished in two-tone Azure Blue, the oil tank and battery tool box having a Pearl Grey finish.

Super Profile

C3. Right-hand side view of the power unit, illustrating the twin 'chopped off' Amal Monobloc carburettors and remote, flexibly-mounted TT float bowl. This model specified a manual control Lucas K2FC 'Red Label' magneto, whereas subsequent T120 models up to 1963, when twin contact breakers were introduced, were fitted with magneto auto-advance units. The 1959 model illustrated here was the only Bonneville fitted with the Lucas E3L dc dynamo and associated voltage regulator. Subsequent models incorporated ac generator equipment.

C4. This left-hand view shows the typically 'Triumph' aspect of the engine, frame, primary drive and exhaust pipe layout. Great attention was always paid by Edward Turner to co-ordination of shape and line, the 'streamlined egg' being the ultimate objective.

Super Profile

C5. Rider's eye view of the neat layout of the instruments and controls. However, the nacelle was only fitted to the Bonneville for 1959, and the tank top parcel grid was discontinued some years later for safety reasons. Note the filler caps on the right-hand side.

C6. Another right-hand side view, again showing the happy blend of the individual components, providing a pleasing and well-balanced integrated design concept. Not a typical achievement of many of the competitors, it was certainly one of the many reasons behind the success of this model.

Super Profile

C7

C8

C7. The 1973 T120 or T140 model was finished in Hi-Fi Vermilion, with Gold scalloped side panels lined in White. The 650cc model was four-speed, with a 5-speed gearbox option, whereas the 750cc T140 was fitted with a 5-speed gearbox as standard specification.

C8. 1974/5 series T140R models to US specification had right-hand gearchange, disc front and drum rear brakes. The finish was Cherokee Red, with Cold White tank top scallops lined in Gold. Machines destined for the USA were fitted with front fork gaiters.

Super Profile

C9. The 1976/7 T140 home and general export model Bonneville. This version was the first new model produced by the Co-operative, and incorporated left-hand gear change and a rear disc brake. It was available in Poly Blue, or Poly Red as illustrated here.

C10. Finished in Aubergine and Gold, the 1968 T120C Bonneville TT model was the last in the series, sporting 1¾ inch diameter straight-through exhaust pipes, stainless steel mudguards and a quilted vinyl twinseat top cover. 54bhp was claimed at 6,500rpm, using 11.2:1 compression ratio pistons, 30mm choke Amal Monobloc carburettors and energy transfer ignition.

Super Profile

C11. Right-hand side view of the 1977 Bonneville Silver Jubilee model owned by John Haynes, illustrating the traditional Red, White and Blue colour scheme on a Metallic Silver ground. Timing, gearbox and primary transmission covers were heavily chrome plated, and the deeply quilted twinseat was finished in dark Blue, with Red piping.

C12. Left-hand side view of the same machine, showing the presentation of the special hand lining of the Silver Jubilee striping on the tank, mudguards and rear chainguard.

C13. Every Silver Jubilee model seat bore this simple legend, which, being in Silver on a Dark Blue background, was an additional but attractive feature.

C14. Even the rear chainguard did not escape the brush of the Triumph paint shop liners. Triumph always had lining on all its paint finishes, never having succumbed to plastic decals or transfers – a fact which US patrons appreciated the most.

C11

C12

C13

C14

Super Profile

C15

C17

C15. A 1978 US specification T140E Bonneville in Crimson and Black, fitted with Amal Concentric Mark II carburettors. Produced specifically to meet strict US exhaust emission regulations, this machine is owned by William Thompson, of Badgworth, Somerset.

C16. The same machine, viewed from the right, illustrating the 'two-into-one-crossover-into-two' complete exhaust system fitted by the owner. Whether it would now meet the equally strict Federal exhaust noise regulations is happily of less concern at present in the UK!

C17. The very essence of Triumph form, presentation and finish, and the spirit of the entire marque, is expressed in this one single shot.

C16

Super Profile

C18. 1979 Bonneville line-up, electronic ignition, new instrument console, rear carrier and a wide range of colour alternatives were now available on home, US and general export models.

C19. American rider's view of the 1979 US Bonneville (double Gold lines a differentiating feature from the previous year). The new instrument console is visible in this shot.

C20. This 1961 Bonneville, resplendent in custom paint and chrome, was exhibited under the title 'Purple Passion' at the Cobo Hall, Los Angeles, in 1962.